How to use your Letts Tour Guide

KW-481-946

The best way to see Britain is, for most people, by car. This Tour Guide has been specially designed to lead you—the motorist—to all that is best in its chosen area.

The Tours

There are ten tours in this Guide and each of them covers between seventy and one hundred miles. If you stop and explore all the places mentioned you will find that a single tour will provide a very full day of motoring (particularly in the more mountainous terrain). If you have plenty of time you could take two days to do some of the tours—in other cases you may wish to shorten your trip a little and you can see from the individual tour maps where this is possible. As the tours are all circular, you may of course start and finish at any convenient point. It should be possible to complete the ten tours within 14 days. But if you combine your motoring with country walking (and all the tours pass through places ideal for stopping to walk—or simply to picnic and relax), they should provide you with routes for two or three weeks. A list of places likely to appeal to children is listed at the end of each tour.

The Maps

The maps (one for each tour and a larger one for the whole area) have been designed specially to show clearly all the information you need—without being unduly technical or too detailed. Readers who usually find map-reading difficult will have no trouble in following the direction and the route. The main approach roads to the tours are also indicated. In addition, a 3 miles to the inch motorists map of the area, such as those published by the RAC, will be useful to those who want to vary their tours.

Reference Books

The days and the times of opening for houses, castles and museums mentioned in the tours are given; these are correct at the time of going to press. The most recent information can be obtained from the ABC Travel Guide *Historic Houses, Castles and Gardens* which is published annually each January. Details of museums and art galleries are given in *Museums and Art Galleries in Great Britain* published in July each year. For more detailed information of an architectural and historical nature, refer to *Cathedrals in Britain* and *Castles in England,* published by Charles Letts.

3

In each tour restaurants with a local reputation for simple meals and good service at an economical price are mentioned. Particulars of other hotels, restaurants and inns are given in the annual reference guide *Hotels and Restaurants in Britain* published by the British Tourist Authority. Pubs, taverns and restaurants recommended by local members of the Country Gentleman's Association and other readers will be found, listed by locality, in *The Best of British Pubs*. Campers and caravanners will want to consult *Caravan and Campsites in Britain,* the bestseller which lists more than 2,000 sites so that you can tell at a glance what facilities each offers. Both books are published annually by Charles Letts and are available at most reputable booksellers and newsagents.

Cumbria Tourist Board, Ellerthwaite, Windermere, Cumbria LA23 2AQ; the Northumbria Tourist Board, 9 Osborne Terrace, Newcastle-upon-Tyne NE1 6TH; the North West Tourist Board, The Last Drop Village, Bromley Cross, Bolton BL7 9PZ; and the Yorkshire and Humberside Tourist Board, 312 Tadcaster Road, York, North Yorkshire YO2 2HF, each publish a wide range of descriptive material about the respective areas covered by these tours. Leaflets and folders can be obtained either direct from the appropriate Tourist Board or from any of the many Tourist Information Centres in the Lake District, the Pennines and the Yorkshire Dales.

LettsGuide

Touring
The Lake District
The Pennines and Yorkshire Dales

revised by Harry Loftus

Charles Letts & Co Ltd
London, Edinburgh, München & New York

First published 1969
Completely revised 1974
Further revised 1979
Reprinted, with an Introduction by Kenneth Clarke, 1980
by Charles Letts and Company Limited
Diary House, Borough Road, London SE1 1DW

Designer: Ben Sands
Cover: Ed Perera
Cover photograph: J Allan Cash
Photographs: British Tourist Authority

Maps: Ray Martin

© Text: Charles Letts and Company Limited
ISBN: 0 85097 430 5

Printed in Great Britain by
Charles Letts (Scotland) Ltd

Contents

			Page
		Introduction	6
Tour	1	The Lake District, including Derwentwater and Ullswater	14
Tour	2	The Lake District, including Coniston Water	21
Tour	3	The Lake District, including the Western Dales	28
Tour	4	The Vale of Eden and Weardale	34
Tour	5	Hadrian's Wall, the Upper Pennines and Tynedale	40
Tour	6	The Pennines, with Teesdale and Swaledale	47
Tour	7	The Yorkshire Dales: Wharfedale and Wensleydale	52
Tour	8	The Yorkshire Dales: Swaledale and Nidderdale	58
Tour	9	The Lower Pennines: Ribblesdale to Lunesdale	64
Tour	10	The Yorkshire Dales: Wensleydale and Ribblesdale	73
		Index	79

Maps

Geological Map   8

Area Map   12 and 13

Tour Maps are on the first or second page of each tour.

Introduction

The following ten tours explore three much-loved areas: the Lake District, regarded by many as the most beautiful part of England, the wild Pennine moorlands reaching north to the unique Hadrian's Wall; and the lovely Yorkshire Dales, with their sweeping valleys and ruined abbeys.

Taken together, the places described comprise a tapestry of English history, beginning with the famous Roman Wall of 120 AD, the traces of the Viking settlements of the tenth century, the building of the Cistercian abbeys in the twelfth century, the later establishment of many pleasing market townships and finally the land enclosures of the eighteenth and nineteenth centuries, which brought about the building of the distinctive stone walls of the Yorkshire Dales.

National Parks

When motoring in the Lake District and parts of Yorkshire and Northumberland covered by these tours, you will soon be aware that you are travelling through National Parks. These are areas of outstanding natural beauty which need to be conserved so that all may enjoy them. There are ten such parks in England and Wales, designated by the Countryside Commission in 1949, and together they cover 10% of the areas of those countries. The designation does not mean that the land is "nationalised" however—it remains in the possession of existing landlords, but any development, such as new building, must be approved by the controlling boards, so that the appearance of the countryside is not spoilt. In fact, two of the biggest landowners in the Lake District are the National Trust (a private charity which looks after historic buildings) and the Forestry Commission.

The Lake District National Park Centre at Brockhole, near Windermere, is described in Tour 1. Information Centres, open from Easter until September, and all with accommodation services, are at: Ambleside, Bowness-on-Windermere, Keswick, Coniston, Glenridding, Hawkshead and Pooley Bridge. The National Park also provides a daily weather advice service by telephone and a caravan and camping advisory service at Windermere. In Yorkshire there are accommodation services at the information centres at Harrogate, Haworth, Knaresborough, Leyburn, Richmond, Ripon and Settle.

Scenery and Geology

One of the attractions of the Lake District is the great variety of scenery in its mountains and lakes, tarns and valleys. And yet this range of scenic beauty is contained within a comparatively small area. It is surprising how different the lakes are in character—compare the lyrical beauty of Derwentwater with its little islands and wooded shores (Tour 1) with the sombre solitude of Wastwater (Tour 3), overshadowed by the awesome Scafell.

The reason for this variety is the different types of rock in the region—in particular the three main types: Skiddaw Slates, Borrowdale Volcanics and Silurian shales and sandstones. In the north, the oldest rocks in the district, the Ordovician Skiddaw Slates, are found in the area between Keswick and Cockermouth. In the mountainous region to the south of Keswick but north of Windermere are the Borrowdale Volcanics which have influenced the scenery greatly because, as an early writer said: "All our fine towering crags belong to the volcanic group and most of the cascades among the lakes fall over it. There are some lofty precipices among the Skiddaw Slates, but because of the crumpling nature of the rocks they present none of the bold colossal features which the central mountains have."

In the lower part of Borrowdale (Tour 1) the contrasting scenery associated with these two rock types can be clearly seen: the precipitous slopes of Walla Crag and Falcon Crag (Borrowdale Volcanics).

Farther south surrounding Lake Windermere and Coniston Water are the slightly younger Silvurian shales, slates, sandstones and limestones.

The mountains in the Lake District were shaped by glaciation during the Ice Age. Glaciers moving slowly towards the sea carved out great U-shaped valleys and carried huge boulders and other rock debris (moraine) which scraped the rocks on the valley sides. The scars left by this action can be seen clearly to this day.

At the end of the Ice Age the valleys became blocked by moraine deposited by the melting glaciers and the famous mountain lakes were formed.

Westwards on the coast, and on the coastal strip south of Lancaster (including the Blackpool area), are a succession of Triassic sediments—the Bunter and Keuper Sandstones and the Keuper Marls.

Trees and Plants

The Ice Age had another important influence: it swept away all previous vegetation in the Lake District, leaving bare rocks. The still-bare rocks in the uplands have remained thus for 10 000 years. Recent scientific research (using pollen analysis) shows that by about 5 000 BC thick forest, mainly of oak and elm, had spread to a height of some 2 000 ft. on the hillsides. Then, about 3 000 BC, there was a dramatic drop in the number of trees, particularly of elms, while the evidence of grass growth increased. The reason was

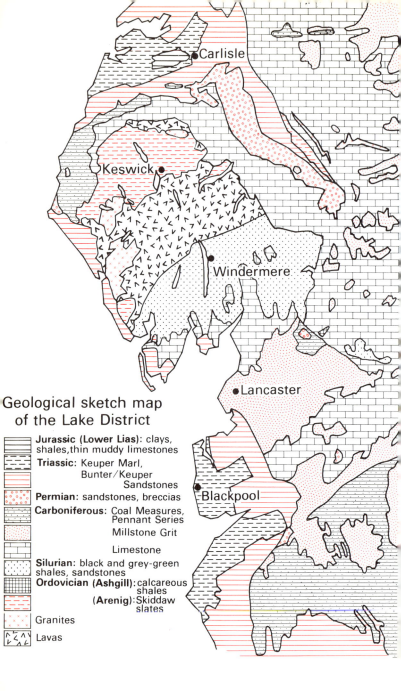

Geological sketch map of the Lake District

Jurassic (Lower Lias): clays, shales, thin muddy limestones

Triassic: Keuper Marl, Bunter/Keuper Sandstones

Permian: sandstones, breccias

Carboniferous: Coal Measures, Pennant Series

Millstone Grit

Limestone

Silurian: black and grey-green shales, sandstones

Ordovician (Ashgill): calcareous shales

(Arenig): Skiddaw slates

Granites

Lavas

Carlisle

Keswick

Windermere

Lancaster

Blackpool

that by axe and fire, Neolithic forest farmers were clearing woodland to create grazing land for their animals.

This process has been reversed in the last 300-400 years, when landowners began planting trees in big numbers, introducing many of the exotic species to be seen around Windermere and which seem so natural in the lakeside scene. The Forestry Commission has now continued the tree-planting programme in the district. The largest forests in their care are at Thornthwaite, Ennerdale and Grizedale. The Commission has an open attitude to public access to their forests and you will find adequate parking facilities, well-marked forest walks, and welcoming information centres on their lands.

Early Dwellers

One of the most interesting recent discoveries, relating to the Neolithic Period of 2500 BC, are the stone-axe factories in the vicinity of Langdale and Sca Fell (see Tour 3). The axes, of Borrowdale Volcanic rock, have been found in distant parts of Britain, and it is assumed that they were used in trade. Other survivals from prehistoric times are ancient stone circles. A fine example can be seen at Castlerigg, near Keswick (Tour 3). Moving on two thousand years to the time of the Roman occupation, the remains of a Roman fort, Hardknott Castle may be viewed at the top of Hardknott Pass (Tour 3). If you look closely you may make out the ancient parade ground levelled out of the hillside above the castle. That tour in fact follows the old Roman road from Hardknott to Ambleside.

The Anglians settled in farms in the Lake District from about the seventh century and a peaceful era can be imagined until the Vikings came in from the east in the tenth century. They did not conflict with the valley-dwelling Anglian farmers however, because they were pastoralists, and reared their cattle, pigs and sheep on the higher hills. It is interesting to note the traces of the Viking settlements in the still existing place-names. You may notice the Norse words "thwaite" (a clearing), "wath" (a ford), "Beck" (a stream), "gill' (a ravine), still exist. They also gave different names to their spring and summer grazing grounds, which you can identify from the place-names "satter", "seet", "sett" or "scale" which mean spring pastures and "airey", "arrow" or "ark" which mean summer pastures. Similar place names on the western side of the Yorkshire Dales will also be found. Viking leaders are also recalled in the name of some of the lakes—Windermere is a corruption of the Viking Vinnunder and Ennerdale of Anundr.

Literary Associations

The Lake District abounds with literary associations, either because writers have lived there or because it has inspired "outsiders" to use it as background for their works. Undoubtedly the greatest of the native writers is William Wordsworth. Born in Cockermouth in 1770 (his birthplace is included in Tour 3), he lived almost all his long life at Rydal and Grasmere (see Tour 1). His descriptive poetry of the region attracted other writers as well as nineteenth century tourists. When Wordsworth settled with his sister Dorothy (who herself wrote a closely observed *Journal*) at Grasmere in 1799 the poet Coleridge moved to Greta Hall at Keswick (see Tour 3). Coleridge's brother-in-law, the poet Robert Southey also lived at the same house. Other writers who visited and wrote about the district include Charles Lamb, Keats, Shelley and Hazlitt.

In more recent days John Ruskin, the great Victorian art critic, went to live at Brantwood on the shores of Coniston for the last 30 years of his life. His house (see Tour 2), full of his geological specimens and paintings, still retains a strong impression of his unusual character.

Probably the best known writer to adults and children alike, Beatrix Potter, lived and wrote at the cottage "Hill Top" at Little Sawrey (Tour 2). She left the cottage when she married, and so it has been preserved exactly as when she wrote and painted there, and you will recognise the rooms and furniture from the accurate watercolours in her classic little books.

Dales—Scenery and Geology

The scenery of the Yorkshire Dales and the Pennines is not so dramatic as that of the Lake District. The Dales are generally more gentle, each dominated by the nature of its eastward- or westward-draining rivers. Stone walls are of course also an outstanding feature of the Dales—most striking when seen from high land, when their patchwork patterns can be best appreciated. Castles abound—at Appleby, Penrith and Raby (Tour 4) at Richmond (Tour 6) and at Knaresborough and Bolton (Tour 8). The remains of Cistercian abbeys may also be seen at Jervaulx and, perhaps the most beautiful of all, the romantic ruins of Fountains Abbey, (both in Tour 7), whose ancient tracery of stone, seen against the smooth green grass of its sheltering valley, is unforgettable.

The geology of the Dales is probably best described starting from the high points of the mountains of Ingleborough and Pen-y-ghent (2 3000 ft.) seen during Tour 10. They rise from a broad plateau of limestone, the edges of the plateau forming a series of fine limestone scars creating precipitous sides of the Ribblesdale valley. Great Scar Limestone is the lowest member of the Lower Carboniferous group of rocks. Above the massive thickness of limestone come the Yoredale series, made up of softer shales and thin limestones. The latter weather quickly, but they are protected

by a top cap of hard Millstone Grit. You can see the limestone
and grit which look like rounded steps on the peaks of
Ingleborough and Pen-y-ghent.

The Great Limestone Scar has often been eroded into almost
rectangular blocks, looking like huge paving stones, and these are
most evident at Malham Cove and Gordale Scar (Tour 10). When
limestone scars occur on the sides of valleys, waterfalls are created
(because the stone below the limestone is impervious). This can be
appreciated best in Wensleydale and Wharfedale (Tours 7 and 10).

The eastern area of the Dales, around Sedbergh and Dentdale
(Tour 6) have a different geology (more akin to that of the Lake
District), consisting of Silurian sandstone, slate and limestone.

Early Dwellers

The Roman Ninth Legion built forts and towns in the Vale of
York, but they seem to have left the troublesome Dales people to
their own devices, building roads and forts to be defended by a
block system. There were forts at Greta Bridge (Tour 6) Bowes
and Brough (both Tour 4) and at Ilkley (Tour 7). A Roman road
ran southwards from the fort at Bainbridge (Tour 10) towards
Lancaster. Bainbridge fort, called *Virosidum* and overlooking the
rivers Bain and Ure, housed some 500 infantry from AD80 until
the end of the Roman occupation. But the fort was largely
destroyed at the end of the second century, presumably by a
native uprising.

Settlement between the seventh and tenth centuries, the Anglians
being joined later by Danes and Norsemen from Ireland, was
similar to that described earlier in relation to the Lake District.
This area suffered, however, from raids from neighbours both
north and south and the scattered farming community did not
develop towns until the sixteenth and seventeenth centuries,
(Hawes for instance did not receive its charter until 1700). Small
textile mills and stone quarries were developed in the eighteenth
and nineteenth centuries but were abandoned later.

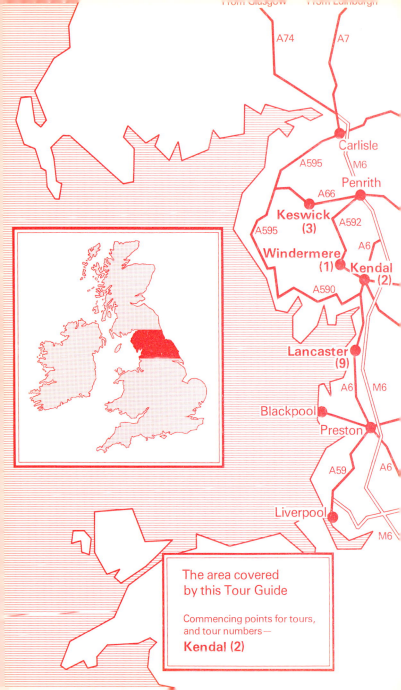

From Glasgow   From Edinburgh

A74   A7

Carlisle

A595   M6

Penrith

A66

Keswick
(3)   A592

A595   A6

Windermere   **Kendal**
(1)   **(2)**

A590

Lancaster
(9)

A6   M6

Blackpool

Preston

A59   A6

Liverpool

M6

The area covered
by this Tour Guide

Commencing points for tours,
and tour numbers—

Kendal (2)

1. The Lake District, including Derwentwater and Ullswater

The first three tours in the Guide cover the Lake District, an area of Lakes nestling beneath wild crags and made famous by the poetry of Wordsworth, Southey and Coleridge. The routes cross and re-cross at various points, and inevitably overlap because of the scarcity of roads built specifically for motor traffic, but the beauty of this area is such that one can never see the majestic hills or the tranquil lakes too often. This tour, starting from Windermere town, takes in six of the lakes. It runs through the lovely valleys of Borrowdale and Patterdale, over the stark passes of Honister and Kirkstone, and includes the tranquil towns and villages of Ambleside, Grasmere, Keswick, Penrith and Troutbeck.

Windermere. As seen from Windermere town Lake Windermere could be a disappointment to a first-time visitor. Though the town of slate-roofed houses sprawls 300 feet above the lake, it offers hardly any views of England's largest lake or of the panorama of spectacular hills round about. To get into the spirit of this tour park the car in Windermere, and then walk along the footpath near to the railway station to the top of the 784-ft. Orrest Head. In the 20 minutes or so that this will take, not only will the full 10½-mile length of Lake Windermere be revealed but, also, you will be able to see the vast expanse of Lakeland fells.

Leave Windermere by the A591 in the direction of Troutbeck Bridge, and after one mile you will see on the left signs indicating the Brockhole National Park Centre. On the opposite side of the road is Briery Close.

Brockhole National Park Centre. The first National Park Centre to be opened, the 19th-century house set in 32 acres of garden and woodland contains an exhibition of models, maps and books connected with the local countryside. The centre is open to visitors daily between mid-March and mid-November.

Briery Close is a beautiful, privately-owned woodland with superb displays of daffodils, roses and flowering shrubs at the appropriate times of the year. Briery Close is open to visitors on certain days in summer, and details can be obtained in Windermere.

Beyond the hamlet of Troutbeck Bridge the road skirts the north-east shore of the lake which, at this point, is thickly wooded. The Low Wood Hotel, on the lake shore, offers one of the loveliest views in Lakeland, and the Coniston Old Man and the Langdale Pikes are seen in their splendour from here. Waterhead is reached in 1 mile.

Waterhead is the terminus of the steamer-ferry from Bowness (described in Tour 2, page 26). To the west is Borrans Park, with a bathing place and a fine view down the lake, and next to this is the Borrans Field, with some remains of the small Roman fort of Galava.

Continue along the A591 for ½ mile to Ambleside.

Ambleside is a busy centre for holidaymakers on Lakeland walking tours. The Bridge House, a 17th-century rough-stone structure built originally as a summer house, spans the Stock Beck and is now a National Trust information centre. St. Mary's Church, built by Sir Gilbert Scott in 1854, has a memorial window to William Wordsworth, and a mural depicting the annual rush-bearing festival held in July. One mile to the east is Stockghyll Force, a lovely waterfall set among woods and reached by the lane from the Salutation Hotel. One mile south of Ambleside and just off the A591 is Stagshaw, a woodland garden rich in rhododendrons, azaleas and flowering shrubs, and giving fine views across Windermere. It is open daily to the public at all reasonable times. The Three Shires Hotel is recommended locally.

Continue along the A591 through the Rothay valley, for 1½ miles to Rydal.

Rydal was for much of his life the home of William Wordsworth. Rydal Mount, his former home set in a 4½-acre garden, is now a museum of Wordsworth relics, and is open daily from early March to mid-January. Rydal Mount and the adjacent Dora's Field, noted for the daffodils of which Wordsworth wrote, offer magnificent views of Rydal Water, which inspired the poet so much. The white-walled Nab Cottage, a short distance along the road from Rydal Mount, was occupied for a brief period by Thomas De Quincey.

The A591 hugs the shores of Rydal Water and Grasmere, one of the smallest and most charming of the lakes, before Grasmere village.

Grasmere was the home of Wordsworth and his sister Dorothy from 1799 until 1808. Dove Cottage, where they lived, is open as a museum Monday to Saturday, April to October; Thursday to Saturday from November to mid-January, and during March. In the churchyard, beside the murmuring Rothay, are the graves of the poet, his wife and sister. Thomas De Quincey, who lived for a time at Dove Cottage, is also buried here. On a Thursday every August the village is thronged with visitors for the Grasmere Sports, games which include fell-racing, hound-trailing and Cumberland and Westmorland wrestling, and which have been held annually since 1852.

Continuing up the Vale of Rothay the A591 reaches Dunmail Raise before descending to Wythburn.

Tour 1
100 miles

━━ ━━ ━━ Unclassified roads

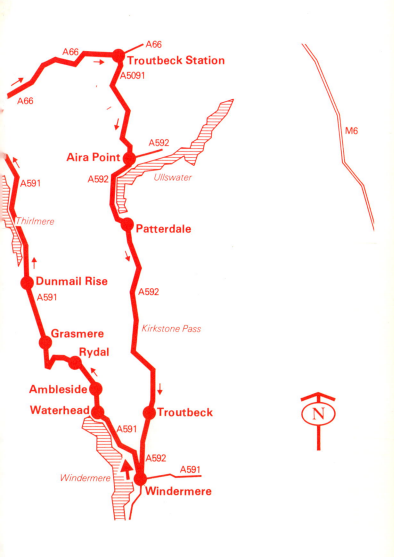

A66

A66

A66 → Troutbeck Station

A5091

↓

A592

Aira Point

A592

A592 Ullswater

M6

A591

Thirlmere

↑

Patterdale

↓

Dunmail Rise

A591

A592

Grasmere

Kirkstone Pass

Rydal

↖

Ambleside

Waterhead

↓

Troutbeck

A591

A592

A591

Windermere

Windermere

N

Wythburn is a hamlet with a tiny 17th-century church, which is at the southern end of Thirlmere. Enclosed by thick plantations and largely hidden from view, Thirlmere was converted in 1879 into a reservoir to supply water to Manchester, a move still deplored after nearly a century by nature-lovers and conservationists. A dam at the northern end of the reservoir is crossed by an unclassified road leading to the west shore of Thirlmere.

The main road (A591) skirts the steep slopes of Helvellyn (3118 ft.) swings to the west of the Vale of St. John and reaches Keswick.

Keswick is described in Tour 3, page 28. It is a convenient stopping place for refreshments, and the Chaucer House and Red House restaurants are recommended locally.

The traveller may decide at this point to take the A66 at Keswick and then follow the directions prior to the Castlerigg entry on page 20.

The route from Keswick is by the B5289 in the direction of Grange-in-Borrowdale, the road skirting the shore of Derwentwater.

Buttermere

Derwentwater is one of the loveliest of the lakes, its surface dotted with small, wooded islands, and its shores a rich mixture of woodland, steep crag and rugged fell. Behind the Lodore Hotel, 3 miles from Keswick, are the famous Lodore Falls, praised by Shelley, but impressive only after a very heavy rainfall.

Continue on B5289 to Grange-in-Borrowdale, a charming village, before entering Borrowdale, and so on to Rosthwaite and Seathwaite.

Borrowdale Many regard this narrow, densely wooded dale as the most beautiful in Lakeland. Look for the Bowder Stone here, a gigantic rock which fell from the crags countless centuries ago, and which appears to be delicately balanced on one edge. There is a ladder which can be climbed to the top. Before reaching Rosthwaite you will see, too, the 900-ft. Castle Crag, a steep cone of rock which appears to fill the vale. A 20-minute walk will take you to the top of this rock, and give you a superb view over Derwentwater. The valley changes its character at Seathwaite, which has the unenviable reputation of being one of the wettest places in England, and opens out into a level, green strath. Ahead, and to the left of the B5289, is the 2949-ft. peak of Great Gable, one of the highest and best-known mountains in the area. Despite its formidable appearance, it can be scaled fairly easily if one is properly-equipped (stout shoes, warm clothes) and experienced.

B5289 now climbs the Honister Pass, a fierce-looking pass with several 1-in-4 gradients, and the summit at Honister Hause is 1176 ft. above sea-level. The descent to the farm of Gatesgarth is no less steep, after which it is possible to admire the gentle beauty of Buttermere, on the left of the road.

Buttermere village, at the north end of the 1½-mile lake, is a pleasant and welcome resting place, particularly for those tired of riding along the narrow switchback roads. A lane from the church leads south to the Sourmilk Gill waterfalls.

B5289 continues along the east side of Crummock Water, another small and tranquil lake, before reaching Low Lorton. From Low Lorton follow an unclassified road for High Lorton where the B5292 is joined for the Whinlatter Pass and Braithwaite. A left turn into the A66 at the village brings you along the west shore of Bassenthwaite Lake, the only 'lake' described as such in the Lake District. From the west shore of Bassenthwaite Lake there are fine views of Skiddaw to the right, and after 4½ miles the lake is rounded and a right turn made into the road signposted Castle Inn. Continue for about 1 mile, crossing the River Derwent by the Ouse Bridge, and at the T-junction at the Castle Inn turn right into the A591. The route now goes down the east side of the lake to Keswick (this criss-crossing of roads is unavoidable in the Lake District) joining the A66 for Threlkeld. About 1½ miles before the village, turn right on to an unclassified road signposted 'Stone Circle'. This leads to Castlerigg.

Castlerigg, an early-prehistoric stone circle, stands on a ridge affording fine views of Skiddaw and Saddleback. Threlkeld, which has the kennels of the Blencathra Foxhounds, has a memorial in the churchyard to 45 foxhounds, 'noted veterans of the chase'.

Follow the A66 until you reach the junction with the A5091, marked to Ullswater, where you turn right, descending Matterdale and Dockray to join the A592 on Ullswater (turn right here).

Ullswater is the second largest of the English lakes (7½ miles long) and is usually regarded as the grandest of them. It consists of three distinct reaches, surrounded by the fells and crags of the Helvellyn and Fairfield ranges. There is a pleasant spot beside the lake where row boats may be hired. Refreshments are available.

The road (A592) runs under Glencoyne Woods before reaching Glenridding, a small village near the head of the lake, and Patterdale.

Patterdale, the village with the same name as the charming dale, is an attractive centre for those climbing the Helvellyn range. St. Patrick, the patron saint of Ireland, is said to have preached here, and 1 mile north of the town is a roadside holy well which he is believed to have used for baptizing converts.

The road (A592) now climbs to the Kirkstone Pass (1489 ft.) which, until the building of the M6 motorway, was an alternative winter route to Scotland when Shap Fell was snowbound. From the Kirkstone Inn, one of the highest, licensed houses in England (cafeteria services too), descend sharply to reach the Troutbeck Valley. Here turn right on to an unclassified road for Troutbeck.

Troutbeck is a delightful little town with a picturesque inn, The Mortal Man, which is recommended locally for meals. Townend, just off the road, is a fine 17th-century yeoman's house, containing carved woodwork and some excellent furniture. Completely naturally lit, it was occupied by the same family from 1626 until 1944. Open daily, except Mondays and Saturdays, between April and the end of October.)

The unclassified road descends to Troutbeck Bridge where the A591 is joined, and a left turn in the direction of Windermere completes the tour.

Appealing to Children

Lakeside and Haverthwaite Steam Railway, Windermere
Brockhole National Park Centre, Windermere
Rydal Mount, Wordsworth museum
Dove Cottage, Grasmere Townend, Troutbeck

2. The Lake District, including Coniston Water

This tour, like Tour 1 and Tour 3, runs through the Lake District, but it includes also the less-crowded area between Lakeland and Morecambe Bay. As well as following the shores of delightful lakes, the route takes in historic towns like Kendal and Cartmel and great houses such as Sizergh Castle and Holker Hall.

Kendal known as the 'auld grey town' because of its many fine houses in grey limestone, is the starting point for the tour. Before the opening of the M6 motorway its narrow streets were often jammed with traffic bound to and from Scotland, and until the 1974 changes in local government structure it was the important administrative centre of Westmorland. Now, Kendal has reverted to its old role as a proud and ancient town—Richard Coeur de Lion granted it a barony in 1189—serving a widespread farming community. George Romney, the portrait painter was born here, and lived for many years in a cottage in Redmayne's Yard, just off the main street. Seven of Romney's paintings hang in the town hall. The parish church of Holy Trinity, one of the largest in England, was built in the 13th century, restored in the 19th century, and is notable for its many chapels. In Stricklandgate, a continuation of the main street called Highgate, is the house where Prince Charles Stuart lodged in 1745-46 on journeys to and from Scotland, and on a green hill to the east of the town are the ruins of the Norman castle where Catherine Parr, the sixth and last wife of Henry was born. Much of this history of Kendal is unfolded in the exhibits in the Abbot Hall Museum and Art Gallery, open daily throughout the year (afternoons only, on weekends), a particularly fine museum in an 18th-century house and the winner of the National Heritage Museum of the Year award in 1973. The Crooklands Inn Motel is recommended locally.

Leave Kendal by the A6 road signposted 'The South and Lancaster'. After 3½ miles along the Kent valley the gates to Sizergh Castle will be seen on the right.

Sizergh Castle, one of the most impressive castles in this part of the country, was built in 1360 as a stronghold against Scots raiders, and it has been the seat of the Strickland family since that date. The castle contains many fine paintings, ceilings and panelling as well as Jacobite relics, and the Tudor great hall added during restorations which continued to the 18th century is impressive. The house is open Wednesday and Sunday afternoons, April to the end of September and Thursday afternoons July and August; the gardens Wednesdays, Thursdays and Sundays, April to September.

Tour 2
65 miles

━ ━ ━ Unclassified roads

A593

Broughton-in-Furness

Grizebeck

A509

Skelwith Bridge

A593

B5286

Tarn Hows

B5285

Coniston

Clappersgate

Hawkshead

Bowness

B5285

Sawrey

B5284

— Ferry

A591

A6

A591

Kendal

A6

Coniston Water

A593

Windermere

Sizergh Castle

A6

Levens Bridge

A6

A5092

Haverthwaite

A590

A590

B5281

B5278

A590

Cartmel Priory

Lindale

B5277

B5278

A590

Ulverston

Holker Hall

Grange-over-Sands

N

Continue along the A6. Immediately after Levens Bridge, the splendid Elizabethan lines of Levens Hall, set in 100 acres of parkland, can be seen on the right.

Levens Hall, the largest Elizabethan mansion in the north-west, contains an impressive collection of paintings and of Charles II furniture. In the grounds is the famous topiary garden laid out by the Frenchman Beaumont in 1689, and, unexpectedly, a unique collection of traction engines and fairground engines. On Sundays in summer these are often set in motion. The house is open on Tuesday, Wednesday, Thursday and Sunday afternoons between May and September, and the gardens daily in this period.

Returning to Levens Bridge, turn left into the A590 for Lindale (6½ miles) and then fork left for Grange-over-Sands.

Grange-over-Sands, a sedate little town sheltered by steep, thickly-wooded slopes and favoured as a place for retirement. Kents Bank, 1 mile south, is the point for which travellers aimed when crossing the treacherous sands of the bay, and the nearby Guides Farm has been the home since the 16th century of the 'oversands guides'. The Commodore and Methven restaurants are recommended locally in Grange.

Leave Grange-over-Sands by a hilly, unclassified road for Cartmel.

Cartmel Priory is sometimes described as the 'cathedral city in miniature'. Founded in 1188 by William Marshall, 1st Earl of Pembroke, the gabled gatehouse near the market cross is, apart from the church, one of the few remains of the priory. The church, however, is rich in superb stained glass and lovely carvings.

From Cartmel follow an unclassified road marked to Ulverston toward Holker and turn right along the B5278 for Holker Hall.

Holker Hall, a delightful 16th- to 19th-century country house with beautiful wood carvings, is set in 22 acres of parkland which contains the biggest herd of fallow deer in Britain. There is a deer enclosure, pets' corner and play area for children, and the house and gardens are open Sunday to Friday, Easter to September.

Continue along the B5278 to Haverthwaite. Just beyond the village, turn left into the A590. Follow the signposts to Ulverston, a thriving port in the 18th century until the entrance was choked by silt. A590 continues to Barrow-in-Furness and the industrialised Furness peninsula, but our route out of Ulverston is by the B5281 to its junction with the A5092, turning left towards Grizebeck and Broughton-in-Furness.

Broughton-in-Furness is a small and attractive market town overlooking the Duddon estuary, which attracts many visitors because of the walks through woodlands surrounding the town. Broughton Tower, a local landmark, is a 14th-century pele tower re-built in the 18th century.

Coniston Water

The A593 out of Broughton-in-Furness passes through the lovely Duddon valley to Torver, a small village at the south foot of the Coniston Old Man (2635 ft.), and in 3 miles reaches Coniston.
Coniston, half a mile from the head of Coniston Water, once had a copper mining industry, though it is hard to visualise the superb scenery here as ever being a source of industry. However, the disused mines can still be seen to the north of the village. John Ruskin, who is buried at Coniston Church, lived at Brantwood, on the east shore of Coniston Water, until his death in 1900. Directions are given to the house from the north side of Coniston Water. The house, open Sunday to Friday from Easter to September, contains many of his pictures and furniture, kept as when he lived there. The Ruskin Museum in Coniston, open daily from April to October, also contains many of his MSS, drawings, books and personal relics.

Leave Coniston by the A593 through Yewdale. To the right the B5285 will be seen leading to Tarn Hows, one of the prettiest of the lakes. It is worth making the slight detour for the magnificent views of the mountains to be seen from The Tarns. The A593 continues through Yewdale, over the high shoulder of High Arnside to Skelwith Bridge and shortly before the hamlet of Clappersgate passes White Craggs Gardens.

White Craggs Gardens, open daily all the year round, offer a splendid display of shrubs, heathers and, in season, of rhododendrons and azaleas. There are magnificent views from the gardens, and the car park is free.

From Clappersgate follow the B5286 through Out Gate to Hawkshead.

Hawkshead, an old village of stone cottages, is certainly one of Lakeland's leading beauty spots. The 15th- to 16th-century church contains the private chapel of the Sandys family, and the nearby Grammar School was founded in 1585 by Edwin Sandys, Archbishop of York. Wordsworth attended the school as a boy, and is thought to have stayed as a lodger at Ann Tyson's cottage in a lane near Red Lion Square in the centre of the village. Wordsworth's name is carved on a desk in the school. The picturesque, old Court House, a relic of a pre-Reformation priory, is now Lakeland's Folk Museum of Rural Crafts, and is open daily, except for Mondays and Thursdays, from Easter to October.

Hawkshead is near the head of Esthwaite Water, and our route, on the B5285, follows the east shore of this 1½-mile-long lake to Near Sawrey, passing Hill Top.

Hill Top, the 17th-century former home of Beatrix Potter, lies just off the road, and is popular with visitors eager to see relics of the famous writer of children's books. Many of the cottage's features will be recognised from the illustrations. The house is open daily from April to October.

The B5285 continues to Far Sawrey and Ferry Nab, where there is a ferry carrying 10 cars at a time across Lake Windermere to Bowness. (There are often long delays in summer, but the alternative is a long detour by road).

Bowness, virtually a suburb of Windermere town, is a popular resort with quaint, narrow streets, and is the headquarters of the Royal Windermere Yacht Club. The 15th-century parish church has some fine 13th-to 15th-century stained glass including some with the stars and stripes arms of the Washington family. If a break for refreshment is needed there are many cafés and restaurants in Windermere, including the Sun, Craigfoot, Elleray, Hide-a-Way, The Knoll and Ravensworth, all of which are recommended locally.

Kendal, the starting point of this tour, is 8 miles from Bowness along the B5284 and a similar distance from Windermere along the busy A591.

Appealing to Children

Abbot Hall Museum, Kendal
Sizergh Castle
Levens Hall with its traction engines
Holker Hall and its deer park
Beatrix Potter's home, Hill Top near Sawrey

Hawkshead Village

3. The Lake District, including the Western Dales

This tour includes the lesser-known western part of the Lake District. It takes in the remote Wastwater and Ennerdale Water, as well as the fine old towns of Keswick, Cockermouth (the birthplace of Wordsworth), the valleys of Great and Little Langdale, the head of the Duddon valley, and the green Eskdale to the west. The Roman fort on the Hardknott Pass and the Viking cross at Gosforth can also be seen; but perhaps the most appealing aspect of this tour is the wonderful and constantly-changing character of the mountains themselves.

Keswick, the starting point for this tour, is an ancient market town sheltered by the steep slopes of Skiddaw (3053 ft.) and about ½ mile from the north end of Derwentwater. In the congested Market Place is the Moot Hall, built in 1813, and along Station Road in the attractive Fitz Park is the Fitz Park Museum, open Monday to Saturday, Good Friday to late October. See the various relics of Hugh Walpole and Robert Southey, the fine scale model of the Lake District and the famous 'musical stones'. Near the lower bridge over the Greta are the pencil factories for which Keswick is noted (there is an exhibition hall nearby), and on a hill above is the 18th-century Greta Hall, the home of Robert Southey and of Samuel Taylor Coleridge. Castle Head, a 529-ft. hill south of the town, provides a glorious view of Derwentwater and Bassenthwaite Lake; and Friar's Crag, a headland on Derwentwater, was described by John Ruskin as one of Europe's finest viewpoints. The Cumbrian Steakhouse and Kings Arms Hotel are recommended locally.

Leave Keswick by the A66 in the direction of Threlkeld and Penrith. An unclassified road signposted 'Stone Circle' on the right leads to Castlerigg, an early pre-historic stone circle. Two miles beyond Threlkeld, take the unclassified road to the left signposted 'Mungrisdale'. This road, mainly across open moorland, gives one the chance to stand back, as it were, and to see the majestic panorama of fells and mountains unfolding. On the left, and in the direction of Keswick, is Saddleback (2847 ft.) and behind it Skiddaw (3053 ft.), and so the hills fold and roll in all directions as the road takes us towards Caldbeck. About 3½ miles before Hesket Newmarket, the Horse and Farrier inn will be seen on the right.

Caldbeck is the first village of a reasonable size on this lonely road. Here John Peel, huntsman of the famous ballad, is buried.

Join the B5299 at the village and go west towards Mealsgate, turning left into the A595 for Cockermouth.

Cockermouth, at the junction of the Cocker with the Derwent, is one of the oldest towns in Cumbria. It was the birthplace in

1770 of William Wordsworth. The house, with the original staircase and fireplaces preserved, is open daily, except Thursday afternoons and Sunday, from April to October. Cockermouth Castle in Castlegate, dating from 1134 and complete with dungeons, was besieged and dismantled during the Civil War, but the great gatehouse and the upper wards survive and are open to the public on Mondays, Wednesdays and Saturdays. South of the town is Moorland Close, a farm house where Fletcher Christian, leader of the Mutiny on the Bounty, was born in 1764. The Appletree restaurant in Main Street is recommended locally.

Take the A5086 out of Cockermouth for Ennerdale Bridge, where a narrow and twisting lane descends rather sharply to Ennerdale Water, a remote lake at the impressive entrance to the wild valley of Ennerdale. This is the only Lakeland valley not accessible by car. From Ennerdale Bridge the A5086 continues to Egremont. Here join the A595 to Gosforth; alternatively, a hilly, unclassified road across moorlands runs into the Calder valley to join the A595 at Calder Bridge. Between Calder Bridge and Gosforth the road passes the huge atomic energy power stations of Calder Hall and Windscale.

Gosforth has a remarkable Viking Cross, probably of the late 10th century, in its churchyard, sculptured with a combination of Norse saga and Christian lore.

An unclassified road from Gosforth signposted 'Wasdale Head' runs towards the secluded hamlet of Nether Wasdale and then along the shore of Wastwater, the deepest and the most sombre of the lakes, with magnificent views of the precipitous Wastwater Screes sweeping down to the opposite shore. This road ends at Wasdale Head.

Wasdale Head is a wild-looking village that is the centre for climbers tackling Sca Fell (3206 ft.), England's highest peak. In the churchyard there are reminders of the hazards presented by these mountains, the graves of rock climbers who have fallen to their death.

Return from Wasdale Head, and at Nether Wasdale fork left for Santon Bridge, a hamlet on the Irt. Turn left here along an unclassified road signposted Eskdale and climb through Miterdale Forest. On the descent to the village of Eskdale Green, a footpath on the right leads to Irton Road Station.

Eskdale is one of the few Lakeland valleys without a lake. The upper reaches are enclosed by an impressive semi-circle of mountains that includes Scafell Pike and Bowfell. About ½ mile beyond Eskdale Green is the King George IV inn, and it may be a welcome refreshment stop before tackling Hard Knott Pass. This pass, with its many hairpin bends and 1 in 3 gradients, is more of an adventure than a meandering drive. Though it only reaches to a height of 1291 ft., its narrowness and its poor surface calls for considerable driving care.

29

Caldbeck

Threlkeld

A66

B5299

A66

A591

Keswick

A595

B5299

A595

Cockermouth

A5086

A595

N

Tour 3
74 miles

■ ■ ■ Unclassified roads

Ambleside
A591
Rydal
A591
A593
Skelwith Bridge
Windermere
Dunmail Rise
Wythburn
A591
Thirlspot
A591
Thirlmere
Derwent Water
B5343
Elterwater
Dungeon Ghyll
Wrynose Pass
Hardknott Pass
Ennerdale Water
Nether Wasdale
Eskdale Green
A5086
Ennerdale Bridge
Calder Bridge
Santon Bridge
A595
A595
A595
Gosforth
A5086

*The unclassified road from Eskdale to the pass runs alongside the
Ravenglass and Eskdale Railway, a narrow gauge railway built in
1875 to carry iron ore and now restored as a passenger line. The
terminal station at Dalegarth is to the left of the road. As the road
climbs upwards you will see, unexpectedly, the square fort, with its
three double gateways, of Hardknott Castle.*

Hardknott Castle was built by the Romans in a highly-strategic
position above the pass. This walled and ramparted fort was
occupied in the mid-2nd century and is accessible to visitors at any
reasonable time.

Hard Knott Pass

From the top of Hard Knott Pass there are splendid views of Eskdale and of the Scafell range of mountains; the road then descends to cross the River Duddon before climbing the narrow and steep Wrynose Pass.

Wrynose Pass links the Bowfell range with the Furness range, and there is a Three Shire Stone by the roadside to mark the meeting points of the old counties of Westmorland, Lancashire and Cumberland.

On the left, and shortly after this point, a steep, narrow lane signposted Elterwater descends to join the B5343 at Elterwater village.

Elterwater, fringed by reeds, is not one of the more attractive lakes, but from its shores one can see the Langdale Pikes.

From Chapel Stile the road ascends Great Langdale and passes the new Dungeon Ghyll Hotel before coming to a halt at the Old Dungeon Ghyll Hotel. Dungeon Ghyll Force, between the hotels, is a waterfall in a narrow ravine with sheer rock walls. Since this is the end of the road, there is no choice but to return back along the B5343, until it joins the A593. Here turn left in the direction of Skelwith Bridge and Ambleside. The route from Ambleside to Keswick by the A591, through Dunmail Raise and Grasmere, is covered in Tour 1, but there are some slight variations to increase one's interest.

Dunmail Rise Dunmail, the last king of Cumbria whose defeat in 945 brought Cumberland under Scottish rule, gave his name to Dunmail Raise, and a cairn by the roadside was once thought to mark his grave.

Continue along the A591. An unclassified road on the left signposted 'Public Road Round Lake' goes round the west shore of Thirlmere, the reservoir that supplies Manchester with water, before re-joining the A591 south of Keswick. The best views of the lake are from this minor road, and in the north-west corner is the 1520-ft. Raven Crag, a favourite with rock-climbers. Keswick, the starting point of this tour, is less than 6 miles away.

Appealing to Children

Boating from Keswick
Fitz Park Museum, Keswick
John Peel's grave, churchyard, Caldbeck
The Castle, Cockermouth
Seaside at Seascale, near Gosforth
Calder Hall and Windscale atomic energy stations
Forest walks in Calder valley
Ravenglass and Eskdale Railway at Dalegarth station
Hardknott Castle, Hard Knott Pass

4. The Vale of Eden and Weardale

This tour, starting in County Durham, passes through the
Stainmore Gap in the Pennines to the lovely Vale of Eden, which
it descends all the way to Penrith. It then climbs steeply over one
of the most majestic stretches of the Pennine escarpment to
Alston, and runs through Weardale. Blanchland, a fascinating and
unspoiled village, may be taken in on a detour if time allows.
Otherwise, the route passes through the old and quaint towns of
Bowes, Brough, Kirkby Stephen, Appleby and Penrith. Unlike the
steep, twisting roads covered in Tours 1, 2 and 3, the roads on
this route should allow pleasurable driving at moderate speeds,
with opportunities to park the car and picnic in comfort.

Barnard Castle is a delightful old market town with broad streets
and many 18th-century stone houses. Below the octagonal 18th-
century Market House is the 16th-century town mansion,
Blagroves House, and the King's Head Hotel in Market Place was
used much by Charles Dickens while investigating conditions in
Yorkshire schools. The Castle, now largely in ruins, originally
guarded a crossing point across the River Tees, and was re-built in
1112 by Bernard Baliol, an ancestor of the man who founded
Balliol College, Oxford, and confiscated in 1296 following the
revolt of John Baliol, King of Scotland. The history of the district
can be learned best in the Bowes Museum, one of the finest
museums in Britain, and this imposing palace-like building has,
as well, an excellent collection of paintings, porcelain, tapestries
and other examples of European art. The museum is open daily
throughout the year.

Leave Barnard Castle by the A688 to Bowes.

Bowes, a village in an exposed position, was once the Roman fort
of Lavatrae. In an angle of the fort, and built between 1171 and
1187, there is a Norman keep which can be inspected. Driving
through the village, one can see at the west end a large house
which is said to have inspired Charles Dickens to create his
Dotheboys Hall in Nicholas Nickleby.

*Shortly after leaving Bowes, the A688 merges with the A66, and
follows the line of an old Roman road across the Stainmore moors
to Brough. The bleak, lofty Stainmore Gap, which the A66 crosses,
is one of the few breaches in the Pennine range.*

Brough, like so many villages and towns on this route, has a
history steeped in war and bloodshed. The ruined castle, built in
the 11th century, was the home of the 13th Baron Clifford,
nicknamed 'The Butcher' because of his cruelty in the Wars of the
Roses. It stands on the site of the Roman fort Verterae, and is
open to the public throughout the year. Stage coaches used to
stop here on the long drive from London to Carlisle, with lamps

34

and guards provided on the return journey for the drive across the lonely Stainmore, regarded as the worst coaching road in England.

Leave Brough by the A685 for Kirkby Stephen.

Kirkby Stephen is an attractive town which received its market charter in 1351. A landmark is the 13th-century church of St. Stephen, approached through a large stone portico, and built on the lines of a small cathedral. When Quakers first appeared in the district in the time of Oliver Cromwell, the vicar incited magistrates to take action against them. The town has several fine Georgian houses, and on the outskirts the ruins of Hartley Castle and Pendragon Castle. The Kings Arms Hotel is recommended locally.

Return north along the A685, then turn left into the B6259 for Warcop, a small village on the River Eden, before re-joining the A66 to Appleby.

Appleby, with a history going back before the Norman Conquest, is dominated by a superb castle, over 800 years old, restored by Lady Anne Clifford, Countess of Pembroke, and now a private residence. Lady Clifford's enthusiasm for building and restoring can be seen on all sides of the town, and the St. Anne's Hospital almshouses (1651), St. Michael's Church and the partly-Norman St. Lawrence Church bear her mark. Two crosses, one at each end of Boroughgate, bear Lady Anne's motto—'Retain your loyalty, preserve your rights'. The Grammar School, which originally stood near St. Lawrence Church in the mid-15th century, had George Washington's brothers, Lawrence and Augustine, as pupils. Appleby Fair in June is famous for its horse-trading and as a meeting place for gipsies. The Bongate, Eden Bridge and Copper Kettle restaurants are all recommended locally.

Continue along the A66 through the Vale of Eden, passing through Temple Sowerby.

Temple Sowerby is an attractive village of red sandstone cottages, with a manor house, Acorn Bank. Once the home of authoress Dorothy Una Ratcliff, the 16th- to 18th-century house has lovely walled and herb gardens open daily, except Mondays, April and October.

Continue on the A66 in the direction of Penrith, but fork left on to the B6262 for Brougham Castle.

Brougham Castle is yet another castle once restored by Lady Anne Clifford and probably the most interesting castle ruin in northern England. Built between the 12th and 14th centuries, the Keep, the Pagan Tower and a chapel remain in a good state of preservation, and are open daily throughout the year. On the left of the B6262, just after passing under a small footbridge and almost hidden from view, is St. Wilfred's Chapel, built in 1658.

Continue to the Eamont Bridge.

Tour 4
114 miles

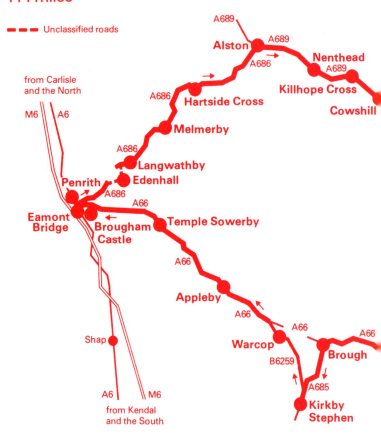

━ ━ ━ Unclassified roads

A689

Alston

A689

A689

A686

Nenthead

A689

from Carlisle
and the North

A686

Hartside Cross

Killhope Cross

Cowshill

M6 A6

Melmerby

A686

Langwathby

Penrith

Edenhall

A686

Eamont
Bridge

A66

Brougham
Castle

Temple Sowerby

A66

Appleby

A66

A66

A66

Shap

Warcop

A66

Brough

B6259

A685

A6 M6

from Kendal
and the South

Kirkby
Stephen

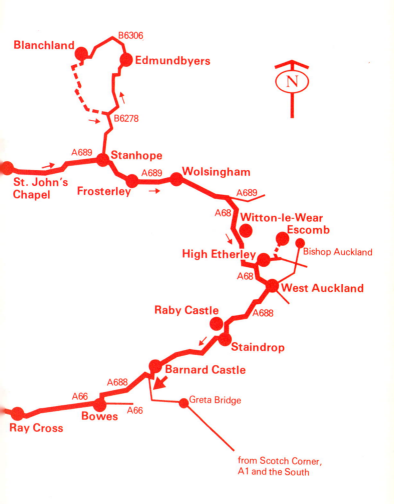

Blanchland
B6306
Edmundbyers
B6278
A689 Stanhope
A689
St. John's Chapel
Frosterley
Wolsingham
A689
A68
Witton-le-Wear
Escomb
High Etherley
Bishop Auckland
A68
West Auckland
Raby Castle
A688
Staindrop
Barnard Castle
A688
A66
Bowes
A66
Greta Bridge
Ray Cross

from Scotch Corner,
A1 and the South

Eamont Bridge the disputed border between England and Scotland before a Papal intervention in 1237. In the village there are two Neolithic earthworks, one known as Arthur's Round Table and the other as Mayburgh, which have puzzled antiquarians for years. The generally-accepted theory is that they were probably burial sites.

From Eamont the A6 runs into Penrith.

Penrith is an attractive market town, once the capital of Cumbria. Penrith Castle, now no more than a ruin set in a public park, was the home of Ralph Neville, Earl of Westmorland, and was later altered by Richard, Duke of Gloucester, before he became King Richard III. St. Andrew's Church, established in the 13th century, was considerably re-built in the 18th century, and in the graveyard is a group of stones, known as the 'Giant's Grave' and the 'Giant's Thumb', which may have been the burial place of one of the Kings of Cumbria. Penrith has many such interesting, historical features—in Bridge Lane the 'Plague Stone' where, in the 17th century, people washed their money in vinegar as a precaution against the plague; the 15th/16th-century inns, the Two Lions and the Gloucester Arms, which may have been frequented by Richard of Gloucester. For present-day travellers the Carlton, Glen Cottage and the Waverley restaurants are recommended locally.

Leave Penrith by returning south along the A6 for a short distance before forking left into the A66 and, after one mile, going left again into the A686 for Melmerby and Alston. The road climbs sharply, with many twists and turns, up the long Pennine escarpment with splendid views over the Vale of Eden to the distant Lakeland fells. The descent to Alston over moorlands is equally sharp.

Alston, a picturesque town of stone houses built on either side of a steep, cobbled main street, stands 1000 ft. above sea level and claims to be the highest market town in England—though Buxton in Derbyshire may dispute the claim. For many years the centre of a lead-mining industry, precision steel products are now manufactured in the town. There are some fascinating old houses with outside staircases in the lanes and yards off the main street, including one dated 1681 with a gallery built over the pavement.

Take the A689 out of Alston for Nenthead.

Nenthead, built as a model village during the 19th century for the local lead miners, has an underground canal designed by John Smeaton. It is one of England's highest villages, standing 1415 ft. above sea level.

From Nenthead the road (A689) climbs steeply to Killhope Cross, and before descending to Weardale at Cowshill, reaches the highest point (2056 ft.) of any main road in England. It also gives inspiring

*views over moorlands in all directions. From Cowshill, continue to
St. John's Chapel and Stanhope.*

Stanhope is a quiet holiday centre with good facilities for walkers.
There is one rarity in the churchyard, a fossilised tree stump found
in a local quarry and believed to be 250 million years old.

*This is the point to decide whether to make the 21-mile detour by
the B6278 to Blanchland by way of Edmundbyers.*

Blanchland, set on the River Derwent, was planned in the early
18th century and can justly claim to be one of Britain's unspoiled
villages. Built round the remains of a 12th-century abbey, the
village square is entered through the abbey gateway of about 1500.
The church and the former abbey storehouse, now the Lord
Crewe Arms, overlook the square.

*The A689 continues to Frosterley, a village long noted for its black
marble which decorates tombs and pillars in churches and
cathedrals throughout the world, and Wolsingham. Four miles
beyond Wolsingham, turn right into the A68 for Witton-le-Wear.*

Witton-le-Wear is a pleasant village above the north bank of the
Wear, with a medieval tower-house re-designed in the 17th
century. Witton Castle, across the river, is a 15th-century tower-
house re-modelled and extended in the 18th and 19th centuries.

*Continue on the A68 to High Etherley and then on to West
Auckland. From the A6073, running east from High Etherley to
Bishop Auckland, a side road descends to Escomb.*

Escomb, a village which has been re-built and restored in recent
years, has one of the best-preserved Saxon churches in the
country, probably dating back to the 7th century.

*From West Auckland follow the A688 in the direction of Staindrop.
Before reaching Staindrop, the road passes the boundary of the deer
park of Raby Castle, and deer can often be seen from the road.*

Raby Castle. The battlemented castle, principally 14th-century,
has a fine collection of paintings and is open on Bank Holidays
and Wednesdays, Saturdays and Sundays in June, July and
September, and daily, except Fridays, in August. The gardens,
covering about 10 acres, are noted for sweet peas.
Continue to Staindrop.

Staindrop is a village with an unusually-long village green. The
green is believed to have been extended over the years as squatters
built cottages, and claimed squatters' rights over the land.

*Barnard Castle, the starting point of this tour, is 6 miles from
Staindrop along the A688.*

Appealing to Children
Bowes Museum, Barnard Castle   Brough Castle
Stanhope churchyard   Deer Park, Raby Castle

5. Hadrian's Wall, the Upper Pennines and Tynedale

This tour follows the course of the great wall of Hadrian, built
from Wallsend, near Newcastle upon Tyne, to Bowness-on-
Solway on the Solway Firth, and one of the most spectacular
relics of Roman Britain. Not only is the Roman Wall of unique
historical interest, it traverses some wild and beautiful country,
crossing the lovely North Tynedale at Chollerford and reaching
the Irthing valley at Gilsland. The tour leaves the Wall near
Lanercost Priory, beyond which there is little to see, goes to the
handsome town of Brampton before ascending to Alston. The
road then crosses the moors and the wooded Allendale to reach
the South Tyne, passing through Hexham and Corbridge.

Hadrian's Wall Before starting this tour it may be useful to know
something about the wall, built between AD 120 and 130
protect the northern frontier of Rome's British province.
Originally 15-ft. high and topped by 6-ft. battlements, it stretched
for 73 miles and was up to 9 feet thick. The wall was patrolled by
soldiers, recruited from many parts of the Roman Empire, from
so-called 'milecastles', barrack buildings 1620 yards or 1 Roman
mile apart. Between the milecastles were two watchtowers at
equal distances, serving the dual functions of observation and
signalling posts. The troops were quartered in 17 large forts placed
at 3- to 7-mile intervals, and these provided granaries, workshops,
living quarters and places of worship for anything between 500
and 1000 men. The wall, finally abandoned in AD 383, was built
along the crests of hills where possible to take advantage of high
ground. A 27-ft.-wide ditch on the northern side of the wall was
intended as a further defensive measure, but when Hadrian visited
Britain in AD 122 he changed his plan and made cavalry
responsible for repelling invaders. For the Roman troops, mostly
recruited from countries with a sub-tropical climate, the posting to
Hadrian's Wall, swept by fierce winds and rain and often
shrouded in mist, must have been one of the least desirable.
After the Jacobite rising of 1745, much of the Roman Wall from
Wallsend to Sewingshields was broken down and used as a
foundation for the Military Road to Carlisle. The first upstanding
sections of the eastern side of the wall are at Heddon-on-the-Wall,
the starting point of this tour.

Heddon-on-the-Wall is a pleasant village on the north side of the
Tyne which is steeped in history. A stone on the river bank dated
1785, and showing the arms of Newcastle, marks the limit for over
600 years of the port of Newcastle. A row of cottages known as
Frenchmen's Row, and dated 1786, was occupied by French
priests fleeing from the Revolution.

*Take the B6318 out of Heddon. On the left will be seen a 100-yard
stretch of well-preserved Roman wall, while the road itself is built
from the remains of the eastern section of Hadrian's Wall. Continue
along the B6318, passing through Harlow Hill before reaching
Halton Chesters and Stagshawbank.*

Halton Chesters Here mounds and ditches remain of the fort of
Onnum. Stagshawbank, a further ½ mile along the road, is an open
common long famous for the large sheep fair held here, and also
the point where the wall was penetrated by the Roman road, Dere
Street.

Continue for 3 miles to St. Oswald's.

St. Oswald's, a solitary 18th-century chapel in an isolated position
north of the Wall, marks the place where St. Oswald, King of
Northumbria, pitched his camp before the battle in AD 634, in
which he defeated King Cadwalla, monarch of Wales.

*B6318 continues through Low Brunton, where there are good views
to the left of the Wall and of a watchtower, to Chollerford and
Chesters.*

Chesters was a Roman cavalry fort, and in the fine park—it is
actually in Chollerford—is the Chesters Museum of items
excavated from the fort. The museum is open daily throughout the
year. Near the bank of the North Tyne there is also a large and
well-preserved bath-house, one of the finest examples in Britain,
and when the river is low, two piers of a bridge built by the
Romans can be seen.

*The B6318 climbs out of the valley to Limestone Corner, where it
is possible to see how the ditch alongside the Wall was cut through
solid rock. From this point there are splendid views north to the
Simonside and Cheviot Hills. The road now runs towards
Sewingshields farm and Housesteads, diverging from the Wall.
Before reaching Housesteads a halt can be made at the remains of
the Temple of Mithras at Carrawburgh which is open daily.*

Housesteads, reached by a footpath from the road, is probably the
most impressive of the remaining forts, and it is possible to see
here the ramparts, gateways, granaries, lavatories and barracks as
they were in Roman times. A mile to the west is a fine example of
a milecastle, and it is worth following the wall on foot from
Housesteads.

The B6318 goes on to the Twice Brewed and the Once Brewed Inns.

Vindolanda, signposted beside the Once Brewed Inn, is part of the
Stanegate, 40 years older than the Roman Wall, a Roman road
built by Agricola linking Corbridge and Carlisle. Excavated
gateways, towers and the headquarters can be seen.

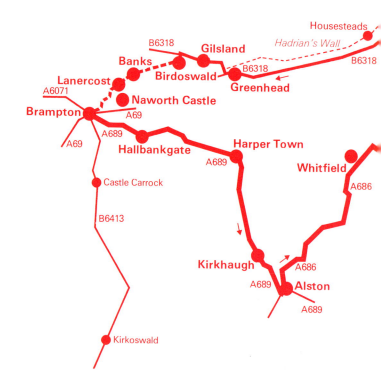

N

Housesteads

Hadrian's Wall

B6318

B6318

Gilsland

Banks

Birdoswald

B6318

Greenhead

Lanercost

A6071

Naworth Castle

Brampton

A69

A69

A689

Hallbankgate

Harper Town

A689

Whitfield

A686

Castle Carrock

B6413

Kirkhaugh

A686

A689

Alston

A689

Kirkoswald

Carrawburgh
B6318
Chollerford
Stagshawbank
Harlow Hill
Heddon-
on-the-
Wall
Chesters
Low
Brunton
Haydon
Bridge
Halton
Chesters
B6318
A69
A69
A69
A69
A686
Hexham
Corbridge
Wylam
Langley Castle
Dilston
A695
B6309
Ovingham
A68
Bywell

Tour 5
100 miles

▬ ▬ ▬ Unclassified roads

43

*Continue along the B6318 through Greenhead, where you cross the
railway and turn right to Gilsland from where you follow the
unclassified road marked to Lanercost.*

Lanercost is a small village approached by a beautiful medieval
bridge and built round a famous 12th-century priory. Founded by
the Augustinian order, the nave was restored in the 18th century
and is now used for services, but other parts of the priory are in
ruins.

*Continue along the unclassified road, passing Naworth Castle, on
the left.*

Naworth Castle, set in a beautiful park, was built in the 14th
century. It passed in 1577 from the Dacre family to 'Belted Will
Howard', featured by Scott in *The Lay of the Last Minstrel.*

*The minor road soon joins the A69. Here turn right to Brampton, 3
miles away.*

Brampton, a handsome town of sandstone buildings on a tributary
of the River Irthing, has an octagonal moot hall in the cobbled
Market Place. The nineteenth century St Martin's church contains
no less than 12 stained glass windows designed and made by
William Morris and Burne-Jones. The large east window is
particularly fine. The White Lion Inn near the moot hall is highly
recommended locally.

*Leave Brampton by the A69 in the direction of Haltwhistle, and
after a short distance fork right into the A689 for Harper Town,
Kirkhaugh and Alston. This road traverses the northern foot of the
Pennines, and provides lovely views on all sides. After passing
through Kirkhaugh, a straggling hamlet, Whitley Castle, a Roman
fort of unknown name, will be seen on the right. From Alston
(described in Tour 4, page 38) take the A686 in the direction of
Haydon Bridge, a lovely road which crosses the moors before
descending to the wooded West Allen valley, finally climbing in zig-
zag turns to the moors again before reaching Haydon Bridge. One
mile before this small town, Langley Castle is passed on the left.*

Langley Castle, a restored 14th-century pele tower, is now used as
a banqueting hall, but can be visited daily during licensing hours.

From Haydon Bridge follow the A69 to Hexham 7 miles away.

Hexham is a delightful agricultural centre. To the east of the
Market Place there is a fine 15th-century moot hall or council
chamber, and the nearby Manor Office or 14th-century prison is
also of interest. The large Priory Church still retains the crypt of
the original church which was built in AD 678; the Saxon throne
in the chancel marks the centre of a medieval circle of sanctuary,
providing protection for any fugitives within a radius of 1 mile
from the throne or stool. A massive staircase from the south
transept once led to the Canons' dormitory. In the town centre

Hexham Abbey: Screen and Pulpit

is The Sele or Seal, originally a monastic enclosure and now a very fine public park. The Beaumont and the Royal restaurants are recommended locally.

Leave Hexham on the A69 in the direction of Newcastle, passing on the right, Dilston Castle, the ruined 15th-century home of the last Earl of Derwentwater, who was executed for his part in the 1715 Jacobite rising. Corbridge lies a short distance ahead.

Corbridge, an interesting village on the north bank of the Tyne, was once the capital of the Saxon Northumbria, and before that the Roman garrison town of Corstopitum. The excavated buildings of the Roman town, including a huge granary—one of the largest Roman buildings discovered in Britain—lie just to the west of Corbridge and, with the interesting museum of excavated finds, is open daily throughout the year. The church at Corbridge, mostly 13th-century, has a unique Saxon porch-tower with a Roman arch.

Leave Corbridge on the A69 and after negotiating a roundabout turn right into an unclassified road for Bywell.

Bywell is an attractive village on the Tyne with two churches, both of them 13th-century, though one of them, St. Andrews', has a Saxon tower. There is also a 15th-century gatehouse in the village.

Continue along the unclassified road to Ovingham, another village with a fine 13th-century church, and on to Wylam, where the birthplace of George Stephenson, of railway fame, can be seen. Take an unclassified road north of Wylam, turning right to rejoin the A69 to Heddon-on-the-Wall, the starting point for the tour.

Appealing to Children

Children are likely to get the most pleasure out of this tour by being allowed to walk along Hadrian's Wall, and to visit some of the Roman forts and milecastles, particularly at Housesteads and Vindolanda.

6. The Pennines, with Teesdale and Swaledale

This tour starts in one of the most attractive towns in North Yorkshire, Richmond, goes northward to the lower part of Teesdale where, if time allows, a detour can be made to the waterfall of High Force. The route then goes across the wild Pennine moorlands to the Vale of Eden, before recrossing the moors to Upper Wensleydale and then over to Swaledale. Towns are rare on this tour, and it will appeal in the main to those who like solitude on a drive. The reward will be a mixture of scenery ranging from the wild grandeur of Swaledale to the open, wooded pastoral peacefulness of Wensleydale.

Richmond, is grandly situated on a steep slope above the Swale. From the top of the 11th-century castle there is one of the finest views in England, a wide panoramic view across the dales to the Vale of York. Dating from the 11th and 12th centuries and one of the earliest to be built in England, Richmond Castle still retains its massive curtain walls, its splendid rectangular Keep and Scollard's Hall. (Open daily throughout the year.) The Market Place, one of the largest in the country, is the centre of the town's life. There are old houses and shops round it, as well as the lovely Georgian Theatre Royal, one of England's oldest theatres, and the Holy Trinity Church from which the curfew is rung each night at 9 o'clock. The Green Howards Museum, covering the history of the regiment, is also in the Market Place.

Leave Richmond by the A6108, turning right into Gallowgate which becomes an unclassified road leading to Kirby Hill and Ravensworth.

Ravensworth is an attractive village built round a large green, near the 14th-century gatehouse and other remains of the once-extensive castle described in Walter Scott's poem 'Rokeby'.

From Ravensworth the minor road continues for 1 mile to the A66. Here turn left to Greta Bridge, 4 miles away.

Greta Bridge is a fine 18th-century bridge by John Carr of York, and near to the entrance of Rokeby Hall associated with Sir Walter Scott. A lane north of the park leads to the meeting of the rivers Tees and Greta, a scene painted by Turner and Cotman. Near by stands the 15th-century Mortham Tower in a lovely setting above the Greta. Charles Dickens stayed in the fine, old 'Morritt Arms' inn, formerly named the 'George'.

A short distance beyond the park, turn right into an unclassified road signposted Barnard Castle.

Egglestone Abbey, set on a knoll above the Tees, was built mostly in the late-12th and 13th centuries, and the ruins can be visited daily throughout the year.

N

A66

Brough

A685

Kirkby Stephen

A685

A683

Sedbergh

A683

Millthrop

A683

B6255

Dent

Newby Head

B6255

High Force B6277

Middleton-in-Teesdale

Mickleton

B6276

Romaldkirk

Cotherstone

A688

B6277

Barnard Castle

A688

Greta Bridge

Egglestone Abbey

A66

Ravensworth

A66

Kirby Hill

A6108

Reeth

Richmond

Thwaite

B6270

Grinton

Buttertubs Pass

Muker

Gunnerside

B6270

A6108

A6136

Hardrow

A684

Hawes

Tour 6

━ ━ ━ Unclassified roads

102 miles

49

Continue past the abbey to the junction with the B6277, and then turn right to follow the signs for Barnard Castle.

Barnard Castle is described in Tour 4, page 34.

Take the B6277 northwards out of Barnard Castle for Cotherstone and Romaldkirk.

Romaldkirk is a delightful village set round a large, irregular green which is overlooked by grey stone almshouses. Lanes lead from the village to reservoirs on the moors above, and the outlook from high up is very impressive.

The B6277 continues to Mickleton, Middleton-in-Teesdale, and, a further 4½ miles up the Tees valley, High Force.

Middleton-in-Teesdale is a quarrying town, where a 16th-century detached bell tower can be seen near a modern church. High Force is a magnificent waterfall, the foaming water gushing over a 70-ft.-high basalt cliff to tumble into the beautiful, wooded glen below.

Return along the B6277 and beyond Middleton-in-Teesdale turn right into the B6276 to climb the desolate Lunesdale for 7 miles before descending to join the A66 a short distance east of Brough. This lonely, minor moorland road runs alongside the river Lune for part of the way, and on the left can be seen the reservoirs above Romaldkirk.

Brough is described in Tour 4.

Continue south along the A685 in the direction of Kirkby Stephen.

Kirkby Stephen (also described in Tour 4, page 35) may be a convenient stopping place for refreshments. The Kings Arms Hotel is recommended locally.

Leave Kirkby Stephen on the A683 for Millthrop and Sedbergh, a stone-built market town famous for its public school. Near the church there is an unclassified road signposted 'Dentdale', and this leads by way of the village of Dent to the dale, one of the smallest and most delightful of the Yorkshire dales.

Dent, with its cobbled main street and colourful houses, is a charming, little town which used to be the centre of the knitted woollen stocking industry. The large church has 13th-century nave arcades, but is otherwise of the 16th century, and there is some good Jacobean woodwork to be found in it. The fountain in the centre of the town is a monument to a noted geologist, Adam Sedgwick, who was born in Dent.

The unclassified road climbs sharply through the upper reaches of Dentdale, with the prominent Whernside (2419 ft.) seen to the right and ahead, and reaches the B6255 where a left turn will lead to the town of Hawes after 7 miles.

Hawes, is described in Tour 10.

Follow the A684 out of Hawes in the direction of Leyburn, but after a short distance turn left into an unclassified road which crosses the river Ure, turning left again and then right to climb steeply to the Buttertubs Pass. Before the climb is made, however, the road to Hardrow, a hamlet near the Hardrow Force, may be followed. After heavy rain the Force is an impressive waterfall.

The Buttertubs Pass, rising 1726 ft. on the watershed between Wensleydale and Swaledale, takes its names from the Buttertubs, a series of deep fissures in the limestone. These are not the largest of the Pennine potholes, but they are the closest to a motor road. On the north side of the pass, it is worthwhile pulling into the side of the road to view the wild scenery that can be seen in every direction, including Great Shunner Fell to the west.

The unclassified road continues to Thwaite, a pleasant hamlet at the foot of Kisdon hill. Here a 2-mile detour can be made by turning left into the B6270 to Keld, a lovely greystone village hemmed in by the fells, with several impressive waterfalls within easy walking distance. Returning to Thwaite by the B6270, the route continues to Muker, once the centre of the Swaledale lead-mining industry, and on to Reeth and Grinton. This stretch of the route reveals that Swaledale is the narrowest, deepest and, possibly, the most remote of the Yorkshire dales.

Grinton was a thriving little village in the 19th century, when the moors above were alive with mining activities, but it is mainly noteworthy now for its attractive three-arched bridge and for its unusually large church. First built by the Normans but mainly in the Perpendicular style, it was in medieval times the burial place for the dead from the whole of Swaledale. A mile before the village, a narrow road on the left leads to prehistoric earthworks, probably dating back to the Iron Age, and from this spot there are superb views of Swaledale.

The B6270 continues towards Richmond for 4½ miles before joining the A6108, and passes the remains of Marrick Priory, a former 12th-century house for Benedictine nuns, now incorporated into the parish church of Marrick.

Appealing to Children

This tour takes in spectacular scenery which will be of interest to adults, but not necessarily to children. However, there is no shortage of places where children can be safely allowed to stretch their legs and to run wild. Three places of interest in Richmond and in Barnard Castle will captivate most children.

The Castle, Richmond
Green Howards Museum, Richmond
Bowes Museum, Barnard Castle

7. The Yorkshire Dales: Wharfedale and Wensleydale

This tour takes in two of the best-loved dales, the long, deep Wharfedale and the broad, pastoral Wensleydale, both with their many delightful villages. It includes, also, the resorts of Ilkley and Harrogate, the interesting monastic remains of Bolton Abbey, Jervaulx Abbey and Fountains Abbey, the impressive ruins of Middleham Castle, and the model villages of Harewood and Ripley, which also has a castle.

Ilkley, the starting point of the tour, is probably best known for its association with the song 'On Ilkla Moor baht 'at' and, to strangers, this could result in a mistaken impression of a pleasant town. Situated on the south bank of the river Wharfe, with a gracious 17th-century bridge spanning the river, Ilkley is popular both as a holiday resort and as a spa. The Manor House Museum (open daily) is situated in a Tudor house built on the site of the Roman fort of Olicana, and its exhibits provide a good insight into the town's long history. All Saints' Church is 16th-century with three Saxon crosses in the churchyard. South-west of the town, above the head of Hebers Ghyll, is the 'Swastika Stone', a carved relic of the Bronze or Iron Age. The moorland road on the south-east passes the Cow and Calf Rocks, a favourite practice slope for rock climbers.

Leave Ilkley by the A65 road in the direction of Skipton, and on the outskirts of Addingham turn right into the B6160 crossing the A59 at Bolton Bridge and on to Bolton Abbey.

Bolton Abbey, with its priory, founded in 1151, is so charmingly situated on the river Wharfe as to have attracted the attention of many artists, including Landseer, designer of the magnificent bronze lions in Trafalgar Square. The priory ruins, open daily, are set among meadows and woods, and the nave, which has been extensively repaired and lengthened, is the parish church. The attraction of the village lies in its setting and in the many pleasant walks around it. Two miles along the A59 in the direction of Harrogate is Beamsley Hospital, a curious circular almhouse dated 1593.

Continue for 2 miles along the B6160, the road following the Wharfe, to reach the ruins of Barden Tower.

Barden Tower, a massive tower-house built in the 15th century, was restored in 1659 by Lady Anne Clifford, then living at Skipton Castle. The ruins, open daily throughout the year, are more impressive because of their beautiful setting. A 17th-century chapel attached to a cottage in the courtyard is worth inspection.

Continue to Burnsall.

Burnsall Every mile of the road through Wharfedale opens up
new vistas, and Burnsall is situated picturesquely on a lovely reach
of the river. The church is 16th-century with a late-Saxon or
Norman font, and the fine old Grammar School was founded in
1602. To the east is Appletreewick (approached by an unclassified
road on the right of the B6160), an attractive hamlet with
Parcevall Hall, an Elizabethan house in beautiful gardens, near
by. The gardens of Parcevall Hall are open daily from Easter to
October.

The dale road (B6160) continues to Linton.

Linton is a delightful village of grey houses grouped round a green,
where the river, now no more than a stream, is crossed by three
bridges—a pack-horse bridge, a clapper bridge and a modern
bridge for traffic. The imposing building in the village is
Fountaine's Hospital, founded in 1721 as an almshouse for six
poor women, but now housing men as well.

*The B6160 continues up the narrowing valley to Kilnsey, a hamlet
under the precipitous buttress of Kilnsey Crag popular with
anglers, and to Kettlewell (which is described in Tour 8)
Continue to Buckden and the Kidstones Pass.*

Buckden, is the highest village in Wharfedale, and the inn provides
the last opportunity for refreshment, before the road climbs
sharply through Cray to the summit of the Kidstones Pass. The
Kidstones Pass is on the watershed between Wharfedale and
Wensleydale, and commands superb views over the Pennine
moorlands.

*The descent through Bishopdale to West Burton is steady, and turn
right when the B6160 joins the A684 to Wensley.*

Wensley, which gives its name to the dale, is a quiet, grey stone
village which was once a thriving commercial centre. First granted
a royal charter in 1202, the town went into decline in 1563
following an outbreak of the plague. The 13th to 14-century
church beside the river, with its Restoration font and 15th-
century screen, is an indication of Wensley's earlier importance.

*Continue along the A684 from Wensley, and fork right into the
A6108 to Middleham.*

Middleham is well-known for its racing stables and attractive in
its own right because of its situation on a hill above the river Ure.
There are several interesting Georgian houses set round the
market-place, but the most impressive building is the 12th-century
Middleham Castle, now largely in ruins, which was once a
stronghold of the Earl of Warwick and a favourite retreat of
Richard III. The massive keep, said to be one of the largest in
England, is enclosed by a 13th-century wall, and is open as an
Ancient Monument on weekdays and Sunday afternoons

Tour 7
94 miles

--- Unclassified roads

N

A1

Jervaulx Abbey
A6108

A6108
Masham
A6108

From Richmond and the North
A6108
Leyburn

Middleham

Wensley
East Witton

West Witton

A684

From Hawes
West Burton
B6160

Kidstones Pass

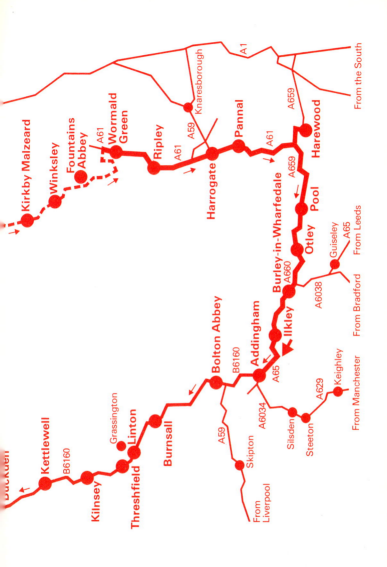

Kirkby Malzeard

Winksley

Fountains Abbey

Wormald Green

A61

Ripley

A61

A59

Knaresborough

A1

Pannal

A61

A659

From the South

Harrogate

Harewood

A659

Pool

Otley

A659

Burley-in-Wharfedale

A660

Guiseley

A65

From Leeds

Ilkley

A6038

From Bradford

Addingham

Bolton Abbey

B6160

A65

Keighley

A629

From Manchester

A6034

Silsden

Steeton

Grassington

Linton

Burnsall

A59

Skipton

Kettlewell

B6160

Kilnsey

Threshfield

From Liverpool

55

throughout the year. Beyond the castle is the moor, where horses from the dozen or so local racing stables can be seen in training.

The A6108 crosses Ulshaw Bridge, a lovely bridge dating from 1674, before reaching East Witton and, 1½ miles beyond the village, Jervaulx Abbey.

Jervaulx Abbey, once a great Cistercian abbey, founded in the 12th century and later dissolved by Henry VIII, has a quiet charm about its ruins if it is less impressive than the remains of Fountains Abbey. Little remains of the church, but the surviving parts of the domestic buildings, in particular the dormitories and the chapter house, are in good preservation, and enable us to form an impression of what day-to-day life in this great monastic house was like. Jervaulx Abbey is open to view throughout the year.

Continue on A6108 to Masham.

Masham is the centre of the Wensleydale cheese industry, much of this pleasant cheese now coming from small factories instead of from farmhouse kitchens. The church, mainly of the 15th century, has a partly-Norman steeple, and in the churchyard is a fragmented Saxon cross.

From Masham follow an unclassified road through Grewelthorpe and Kirkby Malzeard, another cheese-making village with a splendid partly 13th-century church, and on through Winksley turning left and right to reach the B6265 which is crossed, following the sign to Aldfield taking you to Fountains Abbey.

Fountains Abbey, once the wealthiest Cistercian house in England, is certainly now one of the loveliest left behind. Dating from 1132 (the nave and transepts) to 1526 (the tower), the ruins have a majestic splendour which is quite unmatched. The Chapel of the Nine Altars is a masterpiece of rare delicacy, the Refectory can only be described as impressive and the Cellarium, 300 feet long, is breath-taking. The most remarkable feature of all, perhaps, is the wonderful state of preservation of the abbey through the centuries. The abbey is open daily throughout the year, and the adjacent Fountains Hall, a Jacobean mansion with period furniture and tapestries, is open daily from late March to late October. A footpath from the abbey leads for nearly one mile through the impressive grounds of Studley Park, laid out in the 18th century as a formal landscape garden. Ripon described in Tour 8 is 3 miles to the east, and the Old Deanery restaurant is recommended locally.

Leave Fountains Abbey by an unclassified road signposted Markington, and after 3½ miles turn left for Wormald Green before joining the A61. Here turn right for Ripley and Harrogate (both described in Tour 8). From Harrogate continue on the A61, through Pannal to the junction with the A659 where the A61 takes a left bend towards Harewood.

Harewood (pronounced Harwood) is a model village built by John Carr in the late 18th century outside the park of Harewood House. Harewood House, home of the Earls of Harewood, was also designed by Carr, and this splendid mansion with its state rooms, pictures, Chippendale furniture and redecorated Doric Hall and gallery is particularly worth visiting. The park, laid out by 'Capability' Brown, has a bird garden containing 200 species, as well as a cafeteria and children's playground. The 15th-century Harewood parish church is in the park, and it contains a monument to Chief Justice Gascoigne, said by Shakespeare to have committed to prison the Prince of Wales (later Henry V) for contempt of court. Harewood House is open to the public on Wednesdays in February and March and daily from Easter to end October. North of the house are the ruins of Harewood Castle, a 14th-century tower-house.

Return on the A61 in the direction of Harrogate, but turn left into the A659 for Pool and Otley.

Otley is an old market and manufacturing town with a fine 15th-century church with a good Georgian pulpit. In the churchyard is the grim 'Railway Tunnel' memorial to the men who lost their lives building Bramhope railway tunnel between 1845 and 1849. Thomas Chippendale, the noted cabinet-maker, was born in Otley, and a plaque in the Market Place marks the site of his birthplace in 1718.

Follow the A660 out of Otley for Burley-in-Wharfedale, then fork right into the A65 to return to Ilkley.

Appealing to Children

The Manor House Museum, Ilkley
Barden Tower, near Bolton Abbey
The three bridges at Linton
Middleham Castle, Middleham
Fountains Abbey
Harewood House and park

8. The Yorkshire Dales:
Swaledale and Nidderdale

This tour, notable for its many interesting churches and picturesque villages, runs at first through the rich pastoral country of the Vale of York, and takes in the old town of Knaresborough, the Roman remains at Aldborough, the fine Georgian mansion of Newby Hall, and the delightful cathedral city of Ripon. It ascends Swaledale, one of the most beautiful of the Yorkshire Dales, crosses the Pennine moorlands, and turns south to cross the moors again for the lower part of Nidderdale.

Harrogate is a popular spa town which, in recent years, has become well-known as a centre for conferences. The Royal Baths, built in 1897, contain a variety of medicinal-treatment baths and include, also, a large winter garden. The Royal Pump Room (open daily, closed during February) contains the old sulphur well which originally brought the town its fame, and there is, too, a small museum of local history and Victoriana. The town, which has a dignified Victorian charm, is noted for its floral displays, and the Valley Gardens are particularly fine. About one mile west of the town centre, along the Otley Road, are the Harlow Car Gardens, a 60-acre trial ground for experimental gardening, open daily throughout the year and of considerable interest to horticulturalists.

Leave Harrogate by the A61 to The Stray, turning left into York Place and then joining the A59 to Knaresborough.

Knaresborough, situated on a cliff high above the river Nidd, is a sedate town of Georgian houses in narrow streets that will repay closer attention. The remains of the 14th-century Knaresborough Castle, where Richard II was imprisoned in 1399, are impressively sited on a cliff overlooking the Nidd, and are open daily from Easter to late October. On the opposite bank of the river, and reached by the High Bridge, there is the damp and rather eerie Dropping Well, where an assortment of everyday objects are being petrified by the lime in the water dropping from the rock face. Near by is Mother Shipton's Cave, reputedly the birthplace of a legendary prophetess, who predicted: 'World then to an end shall come, in Nineteen hundred and eighty one'. On a more practical note the Conyngham Hall zoo (open daily throughout the year) has a large collection of wild animals and a tropical aquarium.

Leave Knaresborough by the A6055 (B6166) towards Minskip, then turn right into an unclassified road, which crosses the A1 taking you to Aldborough.

Aldborough has extensive remains of the Roman town of Isurium, the most northerly town to be built by the Romans. Portions of the boundary wall can be seen near the church, there are two tessellated pavements at the village inn and a small museum (open daily throughout the year) has a collection of objects unearthed from the site.

Continue along an unclassified road to Boroughbridge.

Boroughbridge, now by-passed by the busy A1, was once an important staging point for the stage coaches plying between London and Edinburgh, and there are some old inns remaining where the horses were stabled. In the market place is a well 250 ft. deep, with a modern canopy. West of the A1 are the Devil's Arrows, three monoliths from 16 ft. to 22 ft. high and probably dating back to the Bronze Age. Why they are here is a puzzle, since prehistoric men are believed to have dragged the huge pieces of millstone grit at least 10 miles to their present site. The Grantham Arms is recommended locally.

Go north along the B6265 for a short distance before turning left into an unclassified road marked to Langthorpe which takes you to Skelton, near which are the gates of Newby Hall.

Newby Hall is a fine Queen Anne house with two wings built by Robert Adam. There is a good collection of statues in a specially-built gallery, as well as some splendid Gobelin tapestries and excellent Chippendale furniture. The grounds covering 25 acres contain a miniature railway and a river on which there are cruises. The house is open on Sunday afternoons only in April and May, afternoons of Tuesday, Wednesday, Thursday and Sunday in June and September, and every afternoon in July and August.

Follow an unclassified road on to Bridge Hewick before turning left on to the B6265 for Ripon.

Ripon is an old market town with narrow, winding streets over which the cathedral looms. Built from the 12th century onwards on the site of an Anglo-Saxon church, the cathedral contains much lovely wood-carving, notably on the bishop's throne and the choir stalls. The focal point of the town is the market square where there is a 90 ft.-high cross, and from here every night at 9 o'clock the town's official horn-blower, the Wakeman or watchkeeper, sounds the curfew. The Wakeman's Museum (open daily, except Wednesdays, throughout the year) is in a house dating back to the 13th century, and contains objects of local and historical interest. There are interesting remains of two ancient hospitals, St. Anne and St. Mary Magdalen in the town, and east of the station the remains of the Sharrow Cross. The Old Deanery restaurant is recommended locally.

Leave Ripon by the A61 going to Thirsk but after a ¼ mile take left turn into the A6108 for West Tanfield.

West Tanfield is an attractive village on a bank of the river Ure. The 15th-century church has fine wood-carvings by Robert Thompson, the Yorkshire craftsman, and the tombs of the

Castle Bolton

Wensley

A684

Leyburn

A684

Aysgarth

B6160

Buckden

B6160

Kettlewell

B6160

Greenhow Hill

B6160

Grassington

B6265

B6265

N

Bolton Bridge

From Manchester

Constable Burton

Patrick Brompton

A684

A684

A684

Bedale

B6268

Snape

Well

West Tanfield

A6108

A6108

Ripon

Bridge Hewick

B6265

Skelton

Boroughbridge

Aldborough

Minskip

A6055

Pateley Bridge

B6165

Summer Bridge

B6165

A61

Ripley

A61

Knaresborough

A59

A59

Blubberhouses

A61

Harrogate

A661

A658

Pannal

Spofforth

From Bradford

Tour 8
84 miles

— — — Unclassified roads

Marmions, who lived at the nearby castle, of which the picturesque 15th-century gatehouse remains.

Leave West Tanfield by an unclassified road for Well and Snape.

Snape Castle was once the home of Catherine Parr, 6th wife of Henry VIII. The ruins of the 15th to 16th-century castle, a stronghold of the Neville and Cecil families, are not open to the public, but the delightful late 15th-century chapel is accessible during daylight hours.

Take an unclassified road from Snape marked to Bedale through Mile House to the junction with the B6268; here turn right for Bedale.

Bedale is a picturesque market town with a wide main street which has held a market for nearly 800 years. Old brick and whitewash houses lining this street provide a pleasing picture. The mainly 13th- and 14th-century church, with its lofty tower arch and vaulted crypt, is one of the finest in North Yorkshire, and facing it is the 18th-century Bedale Hall. The hall now contains a small museum of ancient crafts, and is open on Tuesdays from Easter to late September.

Leave Bedale on the A684, passing through Patrick Brompton, which has a 12th to 14th-century church with an outstanding chancel and nave arcades, and Constable Burton, and then on to Leyburn.

Leyburn, a busy country town, stands above the river Ure and is regarded as the gateway to Wensleydale. The 'Shawl', a 2-mile-long limestone scar reached by a footpath from the town, gives an entrancing view of the dale.

Continue along the A684 to Wensley, where an unclassified road to the right leads to Bolton Castle.

Bolton Castle is a partly-restored stronghold dating back to the late 14th century. Mary, Queen of Scots, was imprisoned here in 1568-69; later the castle was besieged and eventually taken in 1645. Open daily, except Monday, throughout the year, the castle has an interesting Dales Museum including a replica of an early Dales kitchen.

Follow the unclassified road west until it joins with the A684, then turn in the direction of Aysgarth.

Aysgarth is a Wensleydale village with some notable waterfalls in the vicinity. The most noteworthy of these is the Aysgarth Force, reached by a footpath to the north of the church, and in an old corn mill by the falls is an interesting carriage museum (open daily from Easter to late October). The mill, which went out of use for grinding corn as recently as 1968, now houses 60 vehicles, including rare horse-drawn carriages, sleighs and the last woollen dray to be used in Bradford.

Going east of Aysgarth along the A684, turn right after a short distance into the B6160. This narrow, moorland road climbs sharply to Buckden, the highest village in Wharfedale proper, and on the left is the landmark of Buckden Pike.

Kettlewell, one of the prettiest villages of upper Wharfedale, shelters below the 2310-ft. Great Whernside and has a lovely old stone bridge crossing the river Wharfe. This is a favourite centre for rock-climbers, and it is common to see experienced climbers on Kilnsey Crag on fine week-ends. Kettlewell has several inns and cafes, and makes a good halting-place for refreshments.

Take the unclassified road beside the church and follow the east bank of the river, below a series of limestone scars, to Conistone and Grassington.

Grassington is the principal village of upper Wharfedale. It is beautifully situated, with a medieval bridge spanning the Wharfe, and a cobbled market place that is the meeting point for several narrow streets.

Take the B6265 towards Hebden, then over the open Hebden and Appletreewick moors to the Stump Cross Caverns.

Stump Cross Caverns (open daily in summer; week-ends only in winter) are a series of caves and passages beneath the Craven limestone with interesting stalactite formations.

The B6265 continues to Greenhow Hill before descending steeply to Pateley Bridge.

Pateley Bridge is an old-fashioned market town at the entrance to the narrow and beautiful upper part of Nidderdale. Just off the B6265, near Foster Beck, is the Watermill Inn, a former flax mill dating back to the mid-17th century. The wheel, 36 ft. in diameter and weighing about 30 tons, was built in 1800, and is the second largest in existence in Britain.

One mile outside Pateley Bridge join the B6165 for Summer Bridge. To the north of this little village are Brimham Rocks, an outcrop of millstone grit moulded into weird and fascinating shapes by the weather. The B6165 continues to Ripley.

Ripley is a model village with a rare example of a 'Weeping Cross' in the churchyard and with village stocks. Ripley Castle (open on Sundays from Easter to September) has been the home of the Ingilby family since 1350, and is set in fine gardens and grounds.

From Ripley the A61 returns to Harrogate.

Appealing to Children

The Castle   Conyngham Hall Zoo, Knaresborough
The Devil's Arrows, Boroughbridge   Newby Hall grounds
Bolton Castle   Aysgarth Falls Carriage Museum
Stump Cross Caverns   Watermill Inn, Pateley Bridge

9. The Lower Pennines: Ribblesdale to Lunesdale

This tour embraces a wide variety of contrasting scenery: the gentle upper Airedale, the green Lunesdale or Lonsdale, the lonely moors of the Forest of Bowland and the wilder Pennine moors. It starts in Lancaster, a Roman town with great historical associations, takes in the caves and waterfalls near Ingleton, the village of Haworth, famous for its association with the Brönte sisters, and includes the abbey remains at Whalley.

Lancaster is a much-neglected town which motor traffic now by-passes, and through which trains to Scotland travel at high speed. Taking its name from the Roman *castrum* or camp which was sited beside the river Lune at this point, the town has a fine medieval castle, a magnificent priory and several Georgian houses of character. Lancaster Castle (open generally on week-days except when the Crown court is sitting) dominates the town from its position on a hill above the river, and has a Norman keep with many later additions. John of Gaunt, Duke of Lancaster and father of Henry IV was responsible for many of the enlargements, and Elizabeth I added fortifications as a defence against the Armada. The magnificent priory and parish church of St. Mary, which stands alongside the castle, is mainly of the 15th century, though parts date back to Saxon times, and the wood-carvings on the 14th-century choir stalls are among the finest in England. The Old Town Hall in Market Street, a Georgian building, is now the interesting Lancaster Museum (open daily) with local exhibits as well as being the regimental museum of the King's Own Royal Lancashire Regiment. Walk along the tree-lined quay on the Lune, past the Custom House with its graceful Ionic columns, and it is hard to imagine that in the 18th century Lancaster was a port handling a bigger tonnage than Liverpool.

Leave the town by the A6 north, crossing the Lune by Skerton Bridge, and shortly afterwards taking an unclassified road on the right for Halton.

Halton is a peaceful village with a church with a 15th-century tower. In the churchyard stands an 11th-century cross carved with scenes from the Norse saga of Sigurd the Volsung. A mile beyond the village, and near where the road crosses the river, is the Crook o'Lune, a beautiful, wooded ravine that has been painted many times by artists, most notably by Turner. To the north-east is Aughton, a picturesque, hillside village where the thriller writer E. C. Lorac lived during the years before his death in 1958.

After crossing the Lune the road joins the A683, and then continues through the green Lunesdale to Hornby and Melling.

Hornby, on the river Wenning, has the remains of a 16th-century castle whose keep can be seen for miles around. The keep was built by Sir Edward Stanley, who later became Lord Monteagle, after the Battle of Flodden Field in 1513. His coat of arms decorates the unusual octagonal tower of Hornby church, and was put there as a thanksgiving for his safe return from the battlefield. Melling has several charming 18th-century houses, and a 15th-century church containing a set of musical instruments once used to accompany the choir. Tunstall, 2 miles beyond Melling, is the 'Brocklebridge' of *Jane Eyre*.

Continue to Kirkby Lonsdale.

Kirkby Lonsdale, set on a hill above the Lune, is a lovely town much favoured by coach parties of holidaymakers from Morecambe. Among the town's fine buildings are the partly 14th- to 15th-century church, the 17th-century Manor House and the 18th-century Fountain House. The town is the 'Lowton' of *Jane Eyre*. South of Kirkby Lonsdale is the picturesque 13th-century Devil's Bridge spanning the Lune, and beneath it a pool where salmon can often be seen leaping. The Snooty Fox and Copper Kettle restaurants are recommended locally.

Cross the Lune again by the A65, and continue in the direction of Settle by way of Cowan Bridge.

Cowan Bridge is a hamlet on the Leck Beck, and on the right of the road are the old buildings of the Clergy Daughters' School, a school that appears to have had unhappy memories for Charlotte Bronte. The school, now the Casterton Girls' School, has been sited for some years at Casterton, north-east of Kirkby Lonsdale.

Beyond Cowan Bridge continue on the A65 to Ingleton.

Ingleton stands at the junction of two becks, the Greta and the Kingsdale, and is a noted centre of the Craven country of caves and waterfalls. Among the most notable and the most accessible are the White Scar Caves (open daily throughout the year) which are near the B6255 road to Hawes. These are on the lower slopes of Ingleborough (2373 ft.), probably the major landmark of the Pennine hills. From the village there are walks which follow the waterfalls through a series of ravines, and the most impressive after heavy rain are the Thornton Force and the Beezley Falls.

An unclassified road from Ingleton runs south for a $\frac{1}{2}$ mile before joining the A65 to Clapham.

Clapham, a delightful village of grey stone houses in bright gardens, lies in a wooded valley shut in by limestone hills. Ingleborough Cave, reached in $1\frac{1}{4}$ miles by a footpath, has a series of passages and chambers extending for one-third of a mile, and festooned with beautifully-coloured stalactites and stalagmites in a variety of shapes. A mile further along this path is Gaping Gill,

From Kendal and the North

A6 M6 A65 A683

Kirkby Lonsdale

A683 Cowan Bridge

A65

Tunstall

Ingleton

Melling

Hornby

Clapham

A683

Halton Caton

A6

Lancaster

Trough of Bowland

Dunsop Bridge

Whitewell Browsholme Hall

A59

Chatburn

Clitheroe

A6 M6

A59

From Liverpool and the South

Great Mitton

B6246

Whalley

A671

66

Tour 9
112 miles

━ ━ ━ Unclassified roads

65
Giggleswick

Settle

Long Preston

Hellifield

A65

Gargrave A65

Skipton A629 A65

Downham

Blacko

A682 A6068

Colne

Barrowford

Kildwick

Laneshaw Bridge

Haworth

A6033

From Harrogate
and the
Great North Road

Bolton Bridge A59

Addingham

From Leeds
and the
Great North Road

Steeton

Keighley

A629

From Manchester

Settle

a fearsome pothole down which a jet of water hurtles from a height of over 300 feet. This cave is only to be explored in the company of experts.

Continue to Giggleswick on the A65. Beside the Clapham road, 1 mile before Giggleswick is reached, is an unusual ebbing and flowing well.

Giggleswick, on the west bank of the Ribble, is an old-fashioned village with 17th to 18th-century houses and a fine church in the Perpendicular style. The carved pulpit is dated 1680, and there is an ancient reading desk. Giggleswick School, with a prominent domed chapel, is a public school founded in 1512.

Continue to Settle.

Settle, situated at a point where the Ribble flows through the Aire Gap, is a delightful town which combines the dual roles of being a major market centre and a focal point for walkers and pot-holers. It has several attractive 17th and 18th-century houses. The newly opened Pig Yard Museum on Castle Hill houses an excellent collection of archaeological and historic items from the Yorkshire Dales. It is hoped that it will be open daily in summer, and at weekends in winter.

Leave Settle by the A65 which runs down Ribblesdale to Long Preston and Hellifield, and then enters Airedale for Gargrave and Skipton.

Skipton is a pleasant town in which to seek refreshment, and the Midland restaurant is recommended locally.

Leave Skipton by the A629 Keighley road which passes through the Aire valley to Kildwick.

Kildwick, where the Aire is crossed by a bridge that is partly medieval, has a 14th to 17th-century church which is known as the 'Lang Kirk of Craven'. It has an unusually ornate font cover, and in the churchyard there is a 19th-century tomb carved in the shape of an organ.

Continue to Keighley.

Keighley, which stands at the confluence of the rivers Aire and Worth, is a manufacturing town which has carefully preserved its history and character. Cliffe Castle, a 19th-century mansion with formal gardens, a bird garden and a well-wooded park, has been converted to a museum (open daily) with a good collection of local 'bygones', craft workshops and musical instruments. Two miles out of the town, on the Bradford road, is the 17th-century East Riddlesden Hall with the curious wheel windows typical of some West Riding manors. The Hall (open daily from March to October) contains a collection of furniture, pictures and armour, and there is an old tithe-barn.

Leave Keighley by the A629 up the Worth Valley, and in 2 miles fork right for Haworth which is reached in 1 mile.

Haworth, a grey, old-fashioned village with a steep main street, has become a place of pilgrimage to lovers of the Brontë novels. The famous parsonage, to which the Rev. Patrick Brontë brought his family in 1820, is at the top of the main street. It is now the Brontë Parsonage Museum (open weekdays and Sunday afternoons), with relics of Charlotte and Emily Brontë. Their graves are in the churchyard below the old parsonage. The Black Bull Inn, a popular calling place for visitors, is where Branwell Brontë drank himself to death, and on the moors are the ruins of High Withins, the setting for *Wuthering Heights.* The revived Worth Valley Railway, which runs the 5 miles from Keighley to Oxenhope, has its headquarters at Haworth station. It is maintained as a museum and rolling-stock depot (open Saturdays and Sundays and certain weekdays in summer), and includes the largest collection of veteran steam and diesel locomotives in private ownership.

Follow an unclassified road from Haworth church over the wild moorlands of the Forest of Trawden to Laneshaw Bridge, then turn left into the A6068 for Colne.

Colne, on a ridge above the valley of the Colne Water, is a manufacturing town. In Sun Street there is an unusual museum (open Saturdays and Sunday afternoons, May to end September), the British In India Museum, with dioramas, a working model railway, coins, medals and stamps illustrating British government in India up to 1947. The restored 16th-century church has a rare example of mobile stocks in its churchyard.

Take the A56 out of Colne, then fork right into the B6247 for Barrowford. Here the A682 is joined, but at Blacko take a minor road on the left to Downham.

Downham, at the foot of Pendle Hill, is a delightful village of stone-built houses which claims, not without some justification, to be the prettiest village in Lancashire. The Hall, parts of it dating back to the 13th century, was the home for generations of the powerful Assheton family, and it has associations with the Civil War. The 15th-century church has a font given by John Paslew, the last abbot of Whalley.

Continue along the unclassified road to Chatburn, then turn left into the A59 for Clitheroe.

Clitheroe, a pleasant market town that conceals its antiquity, was granted its charter in the 12th century. A ruined Norman keep on a limestone cliff at the end of the main street is all that remains of Clitheroe Castle (open Tuesdays, Thursdays and Saturdays, May to September), but this was one of the greatest strongholds of the Royalists in the Civil War. From the wall round the castle there is a good view of Pendle Hill (1831 ft.) associated with the witches of Pendle. From the summit of the hill it is possible, on a clear day, to see York Minster to the east and the Irish Sea to the west.

Continue along the A59, east of the Ribble, to Whalley 4 miles away.

Whalley, a village on the Calder, is notable for the remains of a 13th-century Cistercian abbey, founded by monks from Cheshire. The remains include part of the chapter house and a splendid 14th-century gateway. The abbey ruins are open daily throughout the year, but the 15th-century Abbot's lodgings, now used as a church conference centre, are not normally accessible to casual visitors. The parish church of St. Mary is mainly 13th-century with some 15th-century additions. There is a wealth of fine, carved woodwork in the church, the choir stalls being outstanding. The churchyard is of unusual interest, containing three Saxon crosses and several gravestones dating back to the 13th century. Two more-recent gravestones are remarkable for recording dates that never existed—April 31, 1752, and February 30, 1819.

John of Gaunt's Castle

Leave Whalley by the B6246 across the Ribble to Great Mitton.

Great Mitton has an interesting church, mainly of about 1300, with a 15th-century tower, 15th- 16th-century woodwork, and family monuments of the Shireburns, who lived at Stoneyhurst, an Elizabethan mansion now a part of the well-known Roman Catholic Stoneyhurst College.

Turn right into the B6243, then take an unclassified road to Browsholme Hall.

Browsholme Hall is a fine Tudor house, altered in the 17th and 18th centuries, with Elizabethan and Stuart panelling, pictures and furniture. It has been the home of the Bowland Forest Rangers for at least 600 years, and contains interesting relics from the forest. It is open Tuesday afternoons, Thursdays, Saturdays and Sundays from Easter to mid October.

From Browsholme Hall follow the unclassified road to Whitewell, a village beautifully situated on the Hodder, then up the valley of the Hodder to Dunsop Bridge, where a left turn is made to ascend to the Trough of Bowland.

The Forest of Bowland is now bare moorland, wild and lonely, but penetrated by attractive valleys. The road climbs from one of these to the Trough of Bowland, a narrow two-mile-long pass reaching about 1000 feet, and linking Lancashire with West Yorkshire. Both the Forest and the Trough are popular with ramblers and cyclists, and the wise motorist parks his car and wanders for a while in one of the many wooded glades. From the highest point of the Trough there are fine views to the left of Morecambe Bay, with the Lakeland hills providing a dramatic backcloth.

Continue on the unclassified road to Abbeystead and the head waters of the river Wyre. The minor road forks right to continue to Lancaster 12 miles away, though an alternative is to take the left fork at Abbeystead, which descends to the A6 near Forton, where a right turn will bring you to Lancaster in 8 miles.

Appealing to Children
Lancaster Castle and the Lancaster Museum
Barry Elder Doll Museum, Judges' Lodgings, Lancaster
White Scar Caves, Ingleton
Ingleborough Caves, near Clapham
Cliffe Castle Museum, Keighley
Brönte Museum, Haworth
Worth Valley Railway Museum, Haworth
Browsholme Hall, near Great Mitton

10. The Yorkshire Dales:
Wensleydale and Ribblesdale

This tour takes in much of Wensleydale as well as a large part of
upper Ribblesdale. Starting from the old market town of Skipton,
it includes many charming villages, the watershed of the Pennine
moorlands, the beautifully-situated remains of Jervaulx Abbey
and the remarkable limestone features of the Craven district. It
is a tour which keeps away from towns in the main, but which
provides impressive views of the desolate splendour of the
Pennine range.

Skipton is a delightful town north of the Aire, with a broad, tree-
lined main street. The great castle of the Cliffords, built in the 11th
century and later, dominates this busy street. Approached through
a gatehouse with rounded towers, the castle (open daily
throughout the year) has a 50-ft.-long banqueting hall, a vast
kitchen with roasting and baking hearths and a dungeon.
Considering that it was under siege for three years during the Civil
War, the remarkable feature of Skipton Castle is its state of
preservation. The Town Hall, also in the High Street, houses the
Skipton Craven Museum (open daily, except Tuesdays,
throughout year; closed Sundays, October to March) with
important exhibits of folk life, lead mining and Roman remains
from the past history of the Craven district. A converted corn mill
in Chapel Hill is the home of the George Leatt Industrial and
Folk Museum (open on Sundays and Bank Holidays), with the
mill restored to what it looked like in 1750, including a working
water wheel. The Midland restaurant is recommended locally.

Leave Skipton by the B6265 (marked to Grassington) for
Rylestone, an attractive village in the limestone gap between the
rivers Wharfe and the Aire. Turn left at Rylestone on to an
unclassified road for Hetton, Airton and Kirkby Malham, where the
road bends north and takes you into Malham.

Malham, an attractive village which gets very crowded during
summer weekends, has that kind of dramatic setting loved by
film producers. Behind the village are sheer rock walls about 300
feet high, and to the east are the impressive cliffs of Gordale
Scar, where waterfalls plunge down into a precipitous gorge.
Malham Cove, about one mile north, is a much-photographed
beauty spot, where the limestone cliffs form a curved back-cloth
to a lovely wooded glen. Once the Aire flowed in a valley above
the cliffs, but now it emerges as a stream at the foot of the cove.
This awesome scenery was produced by earth movements during
the Ice Age, and is a part of what is known as the North Craven
Fault. Malham Tarn, north of the cove, is a quiet, upland lake in
a shallow depression on a wide, green tableland. This is the setting

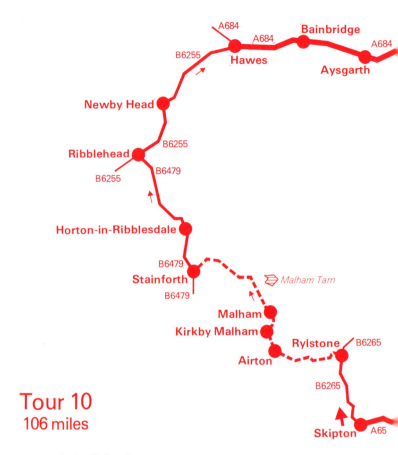

A684

Bainbridge

A684

A684

B6255

Hawes

Aysgarth

Newby Head

B6255

Ribblehead

B6479

B6255

Horton-in-Ribblesdale

B6479

Stainforth

Malham Tarn

B6479

Malham

Kirkby Malham

Rylstone

B6265

Airton

B6265

Tour 10
106 miles

Skipton

A65

━ ━ ━ Unclassified roads

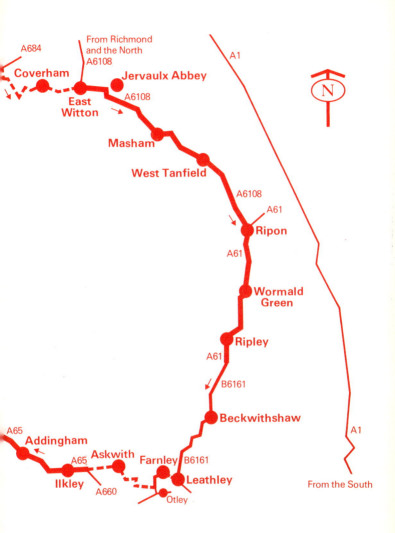

A684

From Richmond
and the North
A6108

Coverham

Jervaulx Abbey

East
Witton

A6108

A1

N

Masham

West Tanfield

A6108

A61

Ripon

A61

Wormald
Green

Ripley

A61

B6161

Beckwithshaw

A1

A65

Addingham

Askwith

A65

Farnley

B6161

Ilkley

A660

Leathley

Otley

From the South

75

Bainbridge

for a part of Charles Kingsley's novel *The Water Babies*, which he wrote at Tarn House on the north side of the lake.

From the tarn take an unclassified road to the left, with many steep and twisting hills, for Stainforth.

Stainforth is a pleasant village with a 17th-century pack-horse bridge over the Ribble.

From Stainforth the route turns north along the B6479 to Horton-in-Ribblesdale.

Horton-in-Ribblesdale is a picturesque, moorland quarrying village with a 12th- to 15th-century church. Quarries scar the fellsides from Helwith Bridge to Horton, and a limestone works towers behind the railway station. The twisted layers of rock to be seen in the district are a magnet for geologists, and ramblers are attracted to the village because of its easy accessibility to the fells. Pen-y-Ghent (2373 ft.) rises to the north-east, and beneath the mountain's slopes are several fine pot-holes, including Alum Pot, Hunt Pot and Hull Pot.

The B6479 follows the course of the upper Ribble valley, climbing to Ribblehead where it reaches a junction with the B6255. Turn right here to Newby Head, a farm on the watershed between the Widdale Beck and the Gayle Beck, and then through the remote Widdale to Hawes, 10 miles away.

Hawes is a grey, old town standing 850 feet above sea level on the river Ure, near the head of Wensleydale. It is the main marketing centre for Swaledale sheep, as well as being a centre for Wensleydale cheese. The wild surroundings of the town are more impressive than the local buildings. South of Hawes, an unclassified road runs through wild country across Fleet Moss towards Langstrothdale. About 1 mile to the north is Hardraw Force, a large waterfall cascading over a limestone ledge, and the road leads over the Butter Tubs Pass.

The A684 from Hawes follows the course of the river Ure through the dale to Bainbridge.

Bainbridge, now a pleasant village built round a wide green, was once the centre of the great Forest of Wensleydale. For 700 years, a hunting horn has been blown each evening from the village green, a reminder of the times when the forest was so dense that the sound of the horn was the only guide for lost travellers. The river Bain flows down through the village from the Semerwater Lake, a one-mile-long lake to the south, and on the east of the river is Brough Hill topped by the remains of a Roman fort. Follow a track from the village towards the Semerwater, and you will be on the remains of a Roman road to Lancaster. The Rose and Crown Inn is highly recommended.

*Continue along the A684 to Aysgarth (described in Tour 8, page 62)
and on to Wensley, but shortly before the village and before the road
crosses the river Ure, turn right along an unclassified road for
Coverham and East Witton.*

Coverham is a hamlet in a delightful position at the foot of the
upper part of Coverdale, with the remains of a 13th-century abbey
built into an 18th-century house. East Witton is a village of old,
greystone cottages built round an attractive tree-shaded green. The
river Cover joins the Ure at this point.

At East Witton the A6108, turning right to Jervaulx Abbey.

Jervaulx Abbey is described in Tour 7. page 56.

*The A6108 runs through the open, lower valley of the Ure to
Masham (described in Tour 7, page 43) and Ripon.*

Ripon (described in Tour 8, page 56) makes a good stopping
place for refreshments on a route which has been mainly through
open country and the Old Deanery restaurant is recommended
locally.

From Ripon take the A61 to Ripley.

Ripley is also described in Tour 8, page 63.

*1½ miles beyond, Ripley, fork right on to the B6161 for
Killinghall and Beckwithshaw and on to Leathley.*

Leathley, a pleasant hamlet on the Washburn near its junction
with the Wharfe, has a church with an early-Norman tower which
retains its original iron-bound door. 1½ miles away by an
unclassified road, is Farnley Hall, the home of the Fawkes family
whose ancestor was the notorious Guy Fawkes. This is an
Elizabethan house with a splendid extension by John Carr of
York. The artist J. M. W. Turner was a frequent visitor here, and
the fine collection of paintings contains many of his works.
As yet, however, it is *still* not open to the public.

*Follow the B6451 to Otley Bridge, turning right for Askwith and
Ilkley.*

Ilkley is described in Tour 7, page 52).

*Leave Ilkley by the Skipton Road, the A65, and Skipton is reached
in 9 miles.*

Appealing to Children
Skipton Castle
Skipton Craven Museum and the George Leatt Folk Museum
Malham Cove
The Wakeman's Museum, Ripon
Ripley Castle
Lindley Wood reservoir, on B6451 north of Farnley

Index

Abbeystead 72
Aldborough 58
Alston 38
Ambleside 15
Appleby 35
Appletreewick 53
Aughton 64
Aysgarth 62,78

Bainbridge 77
Barrowford 70
Barden Tower 52
Bedale 62
Barnard Castle 34, 50
Blanchland 39
Bolton Abbey 52
Bolton Castle 62
Boroughbridge 59
Borrowdale 19
Bowes 34
Bowland, Forest of 72
Bowness 26
Brampton 44
Brantwood 25
Brough 34
Brougham Castle 35
Brockhole National Park Centre 14
Briery Close 14
Broughton-in-Furness 24
Browsholme Hall 72
Buckden Pike 63
Burnsall 53
Buttermere 20
Buttertubs Pass 51
Bywell 46

Carrawburgh 41
Cartmel Priory 24
Castlerigg 20
Chesters 41
Chollerford 41
Clapham 65
Clappersgate 25
Clitheroe 70
Cockermouth 28, 29
Colne 70

Coniston 25
Coniston Old Man 14
Corbridge 46
Coverham 78
Cowan Bridge 65
Crummock Water 20

Dent 50
Dentdale 28

Derwentwater 19, 28
Downham 70
Dunmail Raise 33
Dunsop Bridge 72

Eamont Bridge 38
Edmundbyers 39
Egglestone Abbey 47
Elterwater 33
Ennerdale 29
Escomb 39
Eskdale 29
Esthwaite Water 26

Fountains Abbey 56
Frosterley 39

Giggleswick 69
Glenridding 20
Gosforth 29
Grange-in-Borrowdale 19
Grange-over-Sands 24
Grasmere 15
Grassington 63
Great Mitton 72
Greta Bridge 47
Grinton 51
Grizebeck 24

Hadrian's Wall 40
Halton 64
Halton Chesters 41
Hardknott Castle 32
Hard Knott Pass 32
Harewood House 57
Harlow Car Gardens 58
Harrogate 58
Hawes 77
Hawkshead 26
Haworth 70
Haydon Bridge 44
Heddon-on-the-Wall 40
Hellifield 69
Hexham 44
High Force 50
Holker Hall 24
Honister Pass 20
Horton-in-Ribblesdale 77
Housesteads 41
Hornby 64, 65

Ilkley 41, 78
Ingleton 65

Jervaulx Abbey 56, 78

Keighley 69

Kendal 21
Keswick 18, 28
Kettlewell 53, 63
Kildwick 69
Kilnsey 53
Kirkby Lonsdale 65
Kirkby Malzeard 56
Kirkby Stephen 35
Knaresborough 58

Lancaster 64
Lanercost 44
Langdale Pikes 14
Leathley 78
Levens Bridge 24
Levens Hall 24
Leyburn 62
Lindale 24
Linton 53
Lodore Falls 19

Malham 73
Marrick Priory 51
Masham 56, 78
Melling 65
Middleham 53
Middleton-in-Teesdale 50

Naworth Castle 44
Nenthead 38
Newby Hall 59

Otley 57
Ovingham 46

Parcevall Hall 53
Pateley Bridge 63
Patrick Brompton 59
Patterdale 20
Penrith 38

Raby Castle 39
Ravensworth 47
Richmond 47
Ripley 63, 78
Ripon 59, 78
Romaldkirk 50

Rosthwaite 18
Rydal 15
Rylestone 73

St Oswald's 41
Seathwaite 19
Sedbergh 50
Settle 69
Sizergh Castle 21
Skiddaw 28
Skipton 73
Snape Castle 62
Staindrop 39
Stainforth 77
Stanhope 39
Stump Cross Caverns 63
Summer Bridge 63
Swaledale 51

Tarn Haws 25
Temple Sowerby 35
Thirlmere 33
Thwaite 51
Troutbeck 20

Ullswater 20
Ulverston 24

Vindolanda 41

Warcop 35
Wasdale Head 29
Wastwater 29
Waterhead 15
Wensley 53
West Tanfield 59
Whalley 71
Wharfedale 53
Whinlatter Pass 19
White Craggs Gardens 17
Whitewell 72
Windermere 14
Witton-le-wear 39
Wrynose Pass 33
Wylam 46
Wythburn 18